A HISTORICAL READER

The Holocaust

"I was in a place for six incredible years where winning
meant a crust of bread and living another day.
In my mind's eye, I see those years, and I think of those who
never lived to see the magic of a boring evening at home."

Gerda Weissmann Klein, Holocaust survivor

Table of Contents

PART III: THE CONCENTRATION CAMPS

*Throughout the reader, vocabulary words appear in boldface
type and are footnoted. Specialized or technical words and phrases
appear in lightface type and are footnoted.*

The Situation of Jews in Germany Under Hitler

Dedication

CZESLAW MILOSZ

Czeslaw Milosz (1911–) is a Polish poet who was active in the anti-Nazi movement in occupied Poland during World War II. Milosz's hatred of totalitarianism included the Communist government that established itself in Poland after the war. He fled to the West in 1951. His experience of the century's two great totalitarian movements—Nazism and Communism— led Milosz to devote much of his writing to considerations of ideology, oppression, and blame. In 1980, he was awarded the Nobel Prize in literature. The poem "Dedication" is a tribute to the victims of the Holocaust and a consideration of the value of literature in the face of horror.

You whom I could not save
Listen to me.
Try to understand this simple speech as I would be
   ashamed of another.
I swear, there is in me no wizardry of words.
I speak to you with silence like a cloud or a tree.

What strengthened me, for you was lethal.
You mixed up farewell to an **epoch**[1] with the beginning
   of a new one,
Inspiration of hatred with lyrical beauty,
Blind force with accomplished shape.

Here is the valley of shallow Polish rivers. And an
   immense bridge
Going into white fog. Here is a broken city,
And the wind throws screams of gulls on your grave
When I am talking with you.

What is poetry which does not save
Nations or people?
A connivance with official lies,
A song of drunkards whose throats will be cut in a
moment,
Readings for sophomore girls.
That I wanted good poetry without knowing it,
That I discovered, late, its **salutary**[2] aim,
In this and only this I find salvation.

They used to pour on graves millet or poppy seeds
To feed the dead who would come disguised as birds.

I put this book here for you, who once lived
So that you should visit us no more.

---

[1] **epoch**—the starting point of a period of time, an era, or an age.
[2] **salutary**—beneficial; good for the health.

QUESTIONS TO CONSIDER

1. What does the speaker say about language? Think about
   the contrast between "good poetry" and "bad poetry" in
   the poem.

2. For what purpose does the speaker create this dedication?

The Nuremberg Laws

When Adolf Hitler became chancellor of Germany in 1933,
National Socialism (generally shortened to Nazism) became the
dominant ideology of the state. Nazism was a philosophy based
on racial and ethnic hatred, and its greatest hatred was reserved
for the Jews. The growing hostility and discrimination faced by
Jews in Germany was put into law on September 15, 1935. Two
new laws, known as the Nuremberg Laws, came into effect: one,
the "Reich Citizenship Law," established that Jews could not be
German citizens. The second, the "Blood Law," defined who was a
Jew in the eyes of the law. As the historian Martin Gilbert wrote,
"The Nuremberg Laws made it clear that the Jews were to be
allowed no further part in German life: no equality under the law;
no further citizenship; no chance of slipping back into the main-
stream of German life. . . ." The following is an excerpt from the
Reich Citizenship Law and a record of a case from 1942 defining
the descent and religious status of Mally and Eva Heimann.

FIRST ORDINANCE TO THE REICH[1] CITIZENSHIP LAW

NOVEMBER 14, 1935

On the basis of article 3 of the Reich Citizenship Law of September 15, 1935 *(Reich Legal Gazette I, 1146)* the following is ordered:

Article 1

1. Until the issuance of further regulations for the award of citizenship, nationals of German or related blood who possessed the right to vote in Reichstag elections at the time when the Reich Citizenship Law entered into force or who were granted provisional citizenship by the Reich Minister of Interior acting in agreement with the Deputy of the Führer,[2] are provisionally considered Reich citizens.

2. The Reich Minister of interior acting in agreement with the Deputy of the Führer may revoke provisional citizenship.

Article 2

1. The regulations of Article 1 apply also to nationals who were part Jews *[jüdische Mischlinge[3]]*.

2. Partly Jewish is anyone who is descended from one or two grandparents who are fully Jewish *[volljüdisch]* by race, in so far as he is not to be considered as Jewish under article 5, section 2. A grandparent is to be considered as fully Jewish if he belonged to the Jewish religious community.

---

[1] Reich—term that refers to Germany as an empire or state. The term was applied to Nazi Germany from 1933-1945.

[2] Führer—German word for "leader"; the title that was given to Adolf Hitler.

[3] Mischlinge—The Nuremberg Laws defined some people as only part Jewish and referred to them as Mischlinge. Someone who was half Jewish was a Mischlinge of the first degree. Someone who was a quarter Jewish was a Mischlinge of the second degree.

Article 3

Only a Reich citizen as bearer of complete political rights may exercise the right to vote in political affairs or hold public office. The Reich Minister of Interior or an agency empowered by him may make exceptions with regard to an admission to public office during the transition. The affairs of religious communities will not be affected.

Article 4

1. A Jew cannot be a Reich citizen. He is not allowed the right to vote in political affairs; he cannot hold public office.

2. Jewish civil servants will retire as of December 31, 1935. If these civil servants4 fought for Germany or her allies in the World War, they will receive the full pension to which they are entitled by their last position in the pay scale, until they reach retirement age; they will not, however, advance in seniority. Upon reaching retirement age their pension is to be based on pay scales which will prevail at that time.

3. The affairs of religious communities will not be affected.

4. The provisions of service for teachers in Jewish public schools will remain unaltered until new regulations are issued for the Jewish school system.

Article 5

1. Jew is he who is descended from at least three grandparents who are fully Jewish by race. Article 2, paragraph 2, sentence 2 applies.

---

[4] civil servants—people who are employed in the civil service, the branch of government affairs not military, naval, legislative, or judicial.

2. Also to be considered a Jew is a partly Jewish national who is descended from two fully Jewish grandparents and

a) who belonged to the Jewish religious community, upon adoption of the [Reich Citizenship] Law, or is received into the community thereafter, or

b) who was married to a Jewish person upon adoption of the law, or marries one thereafter, or

c) who is the offspring of a marriage concluded by a Jew (as defined in paragraph 1) after the entry into force of the Law for the Protection of German Blood and Honor of September 15, 1935 (Reich Legal Gazette 1, 1146), or

d) who is the offspring of an extramarital relationship involving a Jew (as defined in paragraph 1) and who is born out of wedlock after July 31, 1936.

Article 6

1. Requirements for purity of blood exceeding those of article 5, which are made in Reich laws or regulations of the National Socialist German Workers' Party and its organizations, remain unaffected.

2. Any other requirements for purity of blood, exceeding those of article 4, may be made only with the consent of the Reich Minister of the Interior and the Deputy of the Führer. Insofar as requirements of this type exist already, they become void on January 1, 1936 unless they are accepted by the Reich Minister of the Interior acting with the agreement of the Deputy of the Führer. Acceptance is to be requested from the Reich Minister of the Interior.

Article 7

The Führer and Reich Chancellor may grant **exemptions**[5] from the **stipulations**[6] of implementory ordinances.

Berlin, November 14, 1935
The Führer and Reich Chancellor
  Adolf Hitler
The Reich Minister of the Interior
  Frick
The Deputy of the Führer
  R. Hess
(Reich Minister without Portfolio)

* * *

Gestapo[7] Office in Düsseldorf/Section 11 B 4 to Reich Security Main Office IV B 4, Berlin, October, 1942

Subject: **Petition**[8] of Emilie Heimann, of German blood, born Adolphs, April 1, 1899, in W.-Elberfeld, married to the Jew Israel Heimann, born January 27, 1900, in W.-Elberfeld, both living in W.-Elberfeld, Sophien Street 12.

Previous: Decrees of May 29 and September 2, 1942 IV B 4 a—847/42

Enclosure: I stapled

The Jewish Community List (critical date October 1, 1935) drawn up by the Jewish Community in Elberfeld and available to my branch office in Wuppertal carries the *Mischlinge* of the 1st degree Eva and Mally Heimann as members of the Jewish religious community. Moreover, their Jewish father, Wilhelm Isr. Heimann designated

---

[5] **exemption**—releasing from duty, obligation, or rule.

[6] **stipulation**—conditions in an agreement.

[7] Gestapo—an official organization of secret police in Nazi Germany.

[8] **petition**—a formal request to one in authority for some privilege, right, or benefit.

them as "Israelite" in the yearly registrations of 1931 and 1932. On the basis of these records, the decision with respect to racial classification was that these Mischlinge of the 1st degree were to be regarded as Jews within the meaning of §5, section 2a of the First Ordinance to the Reich Citizenship Law and that accordingly they had to wear the Jewish star.[9]

The Heimanns deny that they registered their children as members of the Jewish community in Wuppertal or that they permitted them to take part in Jewish religious instruction. During the examination of the records of the Jewish community in Wuppertal it was established that the Jewish community list was put together on the basis of the community's consolidated household list by the Jew Sussmann, now deceased, then employed in the community as a teacher. Sussmann, however, added Jews and Mischlinge who were known to him, but for whom there were no household lists, to the community register. In these cases, he made a handwritten notation and appended any evidence available to the Jewish community. As for the Heimann family as well as seven other persons, there is neither a household list nor any note prepared by Sussmann. It is therefore not possible to provide an **incontestable**[10] answer to the objection of the Heimanns that their children were included in the Jewish community list without their knowledge, since they did not register the children with the Jewish community and prepared no household list. However, inasmuch as today the community possesses neither the household list for the family Heimann nor any writing by Sussmann about them and yet the H. family does appear in the community register, one may suspect that Heimann, who has been employed by the community since 1940 and who had access to all its records,

[9] Jewish star—After September 14, 1941, all German Jews had to wear a yellow Star of David to identify themselves as Jewish.

[10] **incontestable**—beyond dispute or doubt; unquestionable.

destroyed the papers which **incriminate**[11] his family. That there are no records of the seven other Jews can only strengthen this suspicion, since H. relies on the destruction of these records to justify the absence of a listing of his own family.

In view of the above, I request that the appeal of Mrs. Heimann be rejected and that the *Mischlinge* of the 1st degree Mally and Eva Heimann be classified as Jews in accordance with §5, section 2 of the First Ordinance to the Reich Citizenship Law. I hereby return the material sent to me under the decree of May 29, 1942—IV B 4 a 847/742.

Berlin SW 11, January 1, 1943
Gestapo
RSHA IV C 2
Arrest No. H. 16981

Protective Custody Order
First and Second Name: Wilhelm Israel Heimann
Birthday and Birthplace: January 27, 1900 in Elberfeld
Occupation: writer
Marital Status: married
Nationality: German
Religion: Mosaic
Race (to be noted with Non-Aryan): Jew
Residence: Wuppertal-Elberfeld, Sophia Street 12

is taken into custody

---

[11] **incriminate**—show evidence of a crime or fault.

QUESTIONS TO CONSIDER

1. In the eyes of the law, what people were classified as "Jews"?

2. What do you think motivated the Heimanns to file their petition?

3. Why was the Heimanns' petition denied?

Kristallnacht

BY MILTON MELTZER

After the passage of the Nuremberg Laws, the overt persecution of the Jews intensified in Germany. On November 7, 1938, a young German Jew, Herschel Grynszpan, shot an official at the German embassy in Paris. Grynszpan's family had just been deported from Germany to Poland and the young man was outraged by their treatment. When the official died on November 9, a terrifying wave of organized violence broke out against the Jews in Germany. During this infamous Kristallnacht ("Night of Broken Glass"), thousands of Jewish homes, businesses, and synagogues were destroyed throughout Germany. Many Jews were killed and the survivors were forced to pay a large fine in return for the "damage" caused that night.

On November 7, 1938, a seventeen-year-old boy, Herschel Grynszpan, walked up to the German embassy in Paris and shot to death one of its minor staff, Ernst vom Rath.

Young Herschel was the son of one of the 12,000 Jews of Polish origin who a few days earlier had been deported from Germany to Poland. Herschel's father had lived in Germany for twenty-seven years. Like many such immigrants, he had never bothered to seek **naturalization.**[1] Now, overnight, his life had been senselessly smashed.

When Herschel, in Paris visiting an uncle, got a postcard telling of his father's deportation, the act of murder followed. Exactly why the boy did it or what he hoped to achieve by it has never been clear. But the consequences were catastrophic.

The assassination triggered a nationwide **pogrom**[2] in Germany on the night of November 9, the *Kristallnacht* (Night of Broken Glass), which foreshadowed the extermination of the Jews. The assault had been planned by Heydrich and Goebbels at the first news of the shooting of vom Rath. Nazi regional chiefs were instructed by teletype to destroy Jewish shops, synagogues, businesses, and homes. The police were not to interfere, except to protect **Aryan**[3] life and property. Jews, especially rich ones, were to be arrested and confined in concentration camps.

The Party carried out its orders. The torch was set to most of Germany's synagogues; 7,500 shops were ransacked and many destroyed; and hundreds of homes were looted and wrecked. Damage to property, equipment, and stock was estimated at several hundred million marks. At least 1,000 Jews were murdered, and 26,000 were flung into concentration camps.

An American eyewitness described what he saw in Leipzig that night:

> Jewish dwellings were smashed into and the contents demolished or looted. In one of the Jewish sections, an eighteen-year-old boy was hurled from a three-story window to land with

---

[1] **naturalization**—the process of gaining the rights of citizenship.

[2] **pogrom**—the organized massacre of helpless people.

[3] **Aryan**—term used by the Nazis to describe Caucasian non-Jews.

both legs broken on a street littered with burning beds and other household furniture. . . . Jewish shop windows by the hundreds were systematically and **wantonly**[4] smashed throughout the city at a loss estimated at several millions of marks. . . . The main streets of the city were a positive litter of shattered plate glass. . . . The debacle was executed by SS[5] men and Storm Troopers, not in uniform, each group having been provided with hammers, axes, crowbars and incendiary bombs. . . .

A fourteen-year-old boy, M. I. Libau, had gone to bed that night in his home in Berlin. Suddenly, at six o'clock in the morning, the doorbell rang, waking him up. His mother went to the door and opened it. He told what happened then:

I heard the shrill, barking, yelling voices of men. It seemed to me there were at least twenty.

"Are here Gojim or Iwrim [Gentiles or Jews]?" Then I heard my mother's calm voice. "Please speak German. I understand it very well, but if you wish to know whether we are Christians or Jews, we are Jews!"

"Where are the Jews? Where are they?" they yelled. I heard noises of falling furniture and breaking glass. I could not imagine what was happening. I stood behind my bed when one Nazi in full uniform entered the room. He stepped back a fraction of a second when he saw me; then he began to yell, "I'll do nothing to you. I won't do any harm to you."

---

[4] **wantonly**—cruelly; without cause.

[5] SS—Nazis who served as Hitler's bodyguard and as a policing unit of the German army.

Now he stood near me, his face sweating. A smell of bad alcohol came out of his mouth. He took another glaring look at me and began to destroy everything within reach. While he was breaking the closet door, my mother came into the room. He commanded her to hold the clothes for him so that he would be able to tear them better. Desperately my mother called out, "Those are all our clothes! What shall we wear?"

"You wear? Nothing!" he shouted. "You don't need any more clothes! You can go naked now."

It almost broke my heart when I saw him take my father's best suit. "This is my father's best suit," I called out. "Don't tear it! Don't!"

. . . We watched the men destroy the whole apartment of five rooms. All the things for which my parents had worked for eighteen long years were destroyed in less than ten minutes. Piles of valuable glasses, expensive furniture, linens—in short, everything was destroyed; nothing was left untouched. After those ten minutes, the apartment was a heap of ruins.

My mother and I looked at everything without shedding a tear. We felt as if we had lost our minds. The Nazis left us, yelling, "Don't try to leave this house! We'll soon be back again and take you to concentration camp to be shot."

But the Nazis did not come back—then. Mr. Libau, who had been working nights as a forced laborer on the railroad, came home and went into hiding in the cellar of a Christian friend. Many of the family's friends committed suicide that night, some went insane, and some were murdered.

In cold, precise detail, like a bookkeeper's account, the leader of the SS in the town of Geldern reported the action taken locally on orders he had received by telephone:

The first measure was the setting on fire of the synagogue in Geldern at about 4 A.M. By 9 A.M. this was burned down to the foundations. Some bibles in Hebrew characters were taken into safekeeping. Simultaneously the interior fittings of the synagogue in Xanten (a private house) were completely destroyed. There existed two Jewish shops in the Sturm district, the fittings and small stock of which were likewise completely destroyed.

The furnishings of the remainder of the Jews, former cattle-Jews and now earning their living by private means, were totally demolished and rendered unusable, the windows and windowpanes first having been broken in. . . .

By about 11 hours [11 A.M.] all the male Jews fifteen to seventy years of age were arrested by the police and kept temporarily in the local guardhouses. . . . The population took a passive attitude to the demonstrators. . . .

Making a secret report on Nazi party members who had murdered Jews that night, the chief Party judge, Major Walter Buch, revealed how justice had disappeared in Hitler's Germany:

In the following cases of killing Jews, proceedings were suspended or minor punishments were pronounced: Party Member Fruehling, August, because of shooting of the Jewish couple Goldberg and because of shooting of the Jew Simasohm . . . Party Members Behring, Willi and Heike, Josef, because of shooting of the

Jew Rosenbaum and the Jewess Zwienicki . . .
Party Members Schmidt, Heinrich, and Meckler,
Ernst, because of drowning of the Jew Ilsoffer . . .
etc. etc. etc.

Why the *Kristallnacht* pogroms at this moment?
Earlier, if they had wished, the Nazis could have invented any pretext to commit the same barbarism. But not
until now did Hitler feel secure enough to dare a crime
of this magnitude. He had learned he need fear no
opposition from Germans or from the world outside.

Kristallnacht was still another measure of how far
Hitler would go. Coming immediately after his successful intimidation of the major powers at Munich, it tested the German spirit. If his people could swallow this,
they could swallow anything. Was any voice raised in
protest? Neither the Catholic nor the Protestant Church
offered sanctuary to the stricken Jews. Hitler could
smile comfortably and say, "My Germans are united
behind me."

There were notable exceptions. One Catholic
churchman, Bernard Lichtenberg, Provost of Saint
Hedwig's Cathedral in Berlin, spoke out from the pulpit
the morning after the pogrom:

> What took place yesterday, we know; what will
> be tomorrow, we do not know; but what hap-
> pens today, that we have witnessed outside, the
> synagogue is burning, and that, also, is a house
> of God. . . .
>
> In a number of Berlin homes, an anonymous
> inflammatory rag against the Jews is being
> distributed. It says that any German who,
> from allegedly false sentimentality, helps the
> Jews, commits treason against his own people.
> Do not let yourself be led astray by such
> unChristian thoughts, but act according to the

clear command of Christ: "Thou shalt love thy neighbor as thyself."

Because Father Lichtenberg spoke, he served two years in prison. Released, he was seized by the Gestapo and sent to Dachau. He died on the way.

Far more true to the feelings of German Christians at the time was the action of *Landesbischof* Weidemann of Bremen; on November 28, shortly after the burning, pillaging, imprisonment, and murder of the Jews throughout Germany, the state bishop sent this telegram:

TO: THE FUEHRER AND REICHS
CHANCELLOR ADOLF HITLER

THE THREE CHURCHES OF GRATITUDE
IN BREMEN HAVE BEEN INAUGURATED.
THEY BEAR YOUR NAME, MEIN
FÜHRER, IN GRATITUDE TO GOD FOR
THE MIRACULOUS REDEMPTION OF
OUR NATION AT YOUR HANDS FROM
THE ABYSS OF JEWISH-MATERIALISTIC
BOLSHEVISM. I THANK YOU FOR
HAVING ENABLED US TO EXPRESS IN
THESE NEW CHURCHES WHAT IS A
DEEP CONFESSION FOR US WHO ARE
FULLY CONSCIOUS CHRISTIAN NATION-
AL SOCIALISTS.

HEIL, MEIN FÜHRER!

The pogroms of *Kristallnacht* were the unofficial penalty for the death of vom Rath. The next day, Hitler decided to demand the collective punishment of all the Jews. The Fuehrer told Goering that the "Jewish question" must be "coordinated and solved, now, once and for all, in one way or another."

The German bureaucracy swung into action. Measures against the Jews would be planned in an orderly, legal, and systematic way. Pogroms were too messy. The mob turned loose could not always be controlled: *Kristallnacht* had done harm to non-Jewish property and had cost the state some losses. No more. The experts would confer; decisions would be scientifically made; the proper **directives**[6] would be issued; the necessary reports made out and filed.

When casual violence on the streets stopped, many Jews were fooled into believing the worst was over. But it was not; terror simply took another form. Goering imposed the huge fine of 1 billion marks on the Jews; it was the value of 20 percent of all their remaining property. Two billion marks had already been taken from the Jews. The government had collected this "Atonement Payment" and poured it into the rearmament program. Compulsory Aryanization of Jewish businesses moved ahead rapidly. By the year's end, what was left of Jewish business and self-employment was wiped out. It is worth noting that such steps taken "for the good of the German people" at first benefited only one class—the owners of Aryan enterprises. Later the state pocketed a part of the loot.

Before the time of *Kristallnacht*, about a quarter of the Jewish population of Germany had **emigrated**.[7] A year later, more than half the Jews were gone. Three-quarters of those who remained were older people—their businesses, savings, professions, jobs, all gone. They were a dependent community badly in need of relief. It was now that the SD[8] took over the Representative Council of Jews, converted it into the Reich Association of Jews in Germany, and made membership for all "racial" Jews compulsory. It was the

---

[6] **directive**—official guideline that calls for specific actions.

[7] **emigrate**—leave one's country to live elsewhere.

[8] SD—security police established as branch of the SS.

equivalent of a Nazi-controlled ghetto. Public relief was denied the Jews. Unemployed Jews were put to hard labor on construction and reclamation projects, or in arms plants. Jewish wages were slashed, and what was left, taxed. It was slave labor.

"But," said Heydrich,[9] "in spite of the elimination of the Jews from economic life, the main problem remains, namely, to kick the Jew out of Germany."

---

[9] Heydrich, Reinhard (1904-1942)—Hitler's deputy in charge of the "final solution to the Jewish problem."

QUESTIONS TO CONSIDER

1. Why did Hitler wait until the night of *Kristallnacht* to begin his pogrom against the Jews?

2. From the perspective of the German bureaucracy, what went wrong with the pogroms? How did they intend to remedy the problem?

3. Do you think anything like the pogroms of *Kristallnacht* could happen in the United States? Explain why or why not.

Persecution German soldiers shave a Jew's beard, which was a violation of Jewish beliefs.

Anti-Semitism in Germany

Boycotts A Nazi boycott against a Jewish business in Berlin in 1933.
The sign reads: "Germans! Defend Yourselves! Do not buy from Jews!"

▼

▲
Universities Jews were also barred from attending German universities.

Parades At this anti-Semitic parade in Vienna, demonstrators display the wave of anti-Jewish sentiment sweeping Germany and surrounding countries. ▶

German soldiers round up Dutch Jews for deportation to concentration camps.

Roundups Jews march towards a collection point from which they will be shipped to concentration camps.

The Ghettos

The Creation of the Ghettos

BY MARTIN GILBERT AND RAUL HILBERG

Nazi policies caused vast numbers of Jews to flee from Germany in the 1930s. This was actively encouraged by the German government as a solution to what was termed the "Jewish Problem." World War II began in September 1939, and Germany's rapid successes put Hitler in control of a huge portion of Europe by the end of 1940. As emigration was no longer possible, Nazi officials began to search for other ways to remove Jews from Europe. After the conquest of Poland in September 1939, large numbers of Jews—there were more than three million in Poland—were forcibly evicted from their homes to make housing and jobs available for Germans. The evicted Jews were forced into separate areas in the large cities. These areas were known as ghettos and were essentially work camps and holding areas for Polish Jews, who labored to create materials for the German army. The ghettos were supplemented by the building of concentration camps, where able-bodied Jews were sent as slave labor.

In Poland, the isolation of Jews from the rest of the population was being accelerated by regulations forcing Jews to live only in one section of the town. Some of these specially created ghettos were marked by signs on the streets at which they began, and were known as "open" ghettos. Others were surrounded by wooden fences, or barbed wire, or by high walls built for the purpose. Many ghettos were on the outskirts of the town, usually in the dirtiest and poorest suburbs, or in some deserted, or even ruined factory area.

Week by week during 1940, the number of enforced ghettos grew: the Czestochowa ghetto was one of three established in March; the Lodz ghetto was one of two ghettos closed in May. In each ghetto, the German authorities ordered the Jewish Council to carry out its demands, whether for money, forced labor or the reduction in size of the ghettos themselves. In the Lodz ghetto, these responsibilities were carried out by the Chairman of the Council, Chaim Rumkowski, known as the "Eldest of the Jews," who quickly became a controversial figure. On September 6, in Warsaw, Ringelblum noted in his diary:

> Today, the 6th of September, there arrived from Lodz, Chaim, or, as he is called, "King Chaim," Rumkowski, an old man of seventy, extraordinarily ambitious and pretty nutty. He recited the marvels of his ghetto. He has a Jewish kingdom there, with four hundred policemen, three gaols.[1] He has a Foreign Ministry, and all the other ministries, too. When asked why, if things were so good there, the mortality is so high, he did not answer. He considers himself God's anointed.

In the Lodz ghetto, on December 16, the Germans demanded of Chaim Rumkowski that he provide Jews

---

[1] gaol—jail.

for "work battalions." Rumors of this demand prompted fears that those who were not chosen to work might be deported. Four days after the German demand, Rumkowski informed the ghetto representatives that his aim was "to provide work for everybody" inside the ghetto. "Everyone in the ghetto must have work as his passport. If new work battalions are prepared, I will report to the authorities that my reserves are mobilized and waiting to be employed." The enemies of the ghetto were those who launched stories "with the intention of disturbing society's peace." Of these people Rum-kowski declared, "losing his temper," as the Ghetto Chronicle recorded: "I would like to murder them."

Rumkowski told the Jews of the Lodz ghetto, about the Germans: "They respect us because we constitute a center of productivity." For this reason he would present them, Jews and Germans alike, with a plan for the New Year 1942. "The plan is work, work, and more work! I will strive with an iron will so that work will be found for everyone in the ghetto." More than one hundred and sixty thousand Jews were living in the Lodz ghetto as Rumkowski spoke. These included citizens of Lodz, deportees from towns in western Poland and deportees from Greater Germany. Within a week of the Elder pledging work for all, and protection through work, the Germans demanded that ten thousand Jews be found for "resettlement": a special "Resettlement Commission" chose for deportation Jews who had reached Lodz from Wloclawek and its environs the previous October, the families of Jews who had already been sent out of the ghetto for forced labor in Germany, prostitutes, and other so-called "undesirable elements." Beginning on January 13, these ten thousand were ordered to report at the rate of seven hundred a day. Those not reporting would be "forcibly conducted to the assembly point."

In Bialystok, the acting head of the Jewish Council, Ephraim Barasz, felt a new security for the Jews of the ghetto when the German military authorities indicated a possible future order for the manufacture of boots for the German army. Summoning the Council department heads, he told them, as the protocol of the meeting recorded, that he was "certain" that this order for boots "will protect the ghetto from **calamity**."[2] He therefore "demands that industry be assigned top priority in Jewish Council activities." Five months later, the order for boots arrived. "This is sufficient," Barasz told his Council, "to ensure our security and that of the ghetto."

Each ghetto was almost completely cut off from the outside world. News of the different fates of different ghettos was virtually non-existent. Only after the war was it possible to piece together the wider picture. Even as Rumkowski and Barasz spoke with confidence of security through productive work, more and more German, Austrian and Czech Jews were being deported to Riga: some to immediate death, others to labor camps, such as that at Salaspils, where prisoners were hanged "on the flimsiest pretext, after having been tortured before their death," or died "from sheer exhaustion." A thousand deportees from Theresienstadt had been sent to Riga on January 9; four hundred of them being transferred to Salaspils on arrival.

Of the thousand deportees of January 9, only 102 survived the war. Two days later, on January 11, more than fifteen hundred Viennese Jews were seized, and sent likewise by train to Riga. One of them, Liana Neumann, later recalled how "there was no water. The coaches were sealed, and we could not leave them. It was very cold, and we chipped off some of the ice from the windows to have water." Many froze to death on the journey. On reaching Riga, "we were received by SS men, who made us run, and beat us up." Old people, and children, were taken away by force. They were taken away, and killed.

---

[2] **calamity**—great misfortune; serious trouble; misery.

Liana Neumann was sent to work in a hospital; her job was to disinfect the clothing of those Jews who had been killed, for despatch to the German clothes store. With her were a number of local Latvian Jews. "There was a man from Latvia," she later recalled, "who cried out all of a sudden, holding the coat of his little daughter, full of blood."

At Chelmno, the gassing of whole communities was continuing day by day. Gypsies,[3] too, were among the first victims. On January 7, the first of five thousand Gypsies, who had earlier been deported to the Jewish ghetto in Lodz from their encampments in Germany, were taken from Lodz to Chelmno by truck. All were gassed. With them was a Jewish doctor, Dr. Fickelburg, and a Jewish nurse, whose name is unknown. They had been working as a medical team in the Gypsy section of the ghetto. They too were gassed.

On January 9, a thousand Jews from the nearby village of Klodawa were deported to Chelmno. Every one was gassed.

The deportation of Gypsies from the Lodz ghetto having been completed, on January 13 the deportation began of ten thousand Jews from the Lodz ghetto, also to Chelmno, at the carefully controlled rate of seven hundred a day. To lull the deportees with a belief in "resettlement," they had been made to exchange whatever Polish or other money they had into German marks. They were also told that they could either sell their furniture, or leave it "for safekeeping" at the carpenters' shops in the ghetto. Before leaving, each deportee was given a "free distribution" of clothing: warm underwear, earmuffs, gloves, stockings, socks and clogs. They were also given "half a loaf of bread and a sausage for the road."

---

[3] Gypsies—a name for nomadic people found throughout the world.

The Chronicle of the Lodz ghetto recorded with precision the number of deportees: 5,353 men and 5,750 women. The Chronicle only knew that they had been "resettled," not that they had been deported to Chelmno, and gassed.

Diary of Stanislaw Rozycki, containing a monthly budget, probably fall 1941, of his "tolerably well situated" family in the Warsaw ghetto.

Income (Actual)		Expenses (Actual)	
Father's salary	235 Zl.[4]	Rent	70 Zl.
Son's salary	120 Zl.	Bread	328 Zl.
Public assistance	—	Potatoes	115 Zl.
Side income	80 Zl.	Fats	56 Zl.
	435 Zl.	Allotments	80 Zl.
		Fees	11 Zl.
		Electricity, candles	28 Zl.
		Fuel	65 Zl.
		Drugs	45 Zl.
		Soap	9 Zl.
		Misc.	3 Zl.
			810 Zl.

[The family balanced its budget by selling a clothes closet for 400 Zl.]

---

[4] Zl.—Zloty, Polish unit of currency.

Excerpts from monthly report for April 16-May 15, 1941, by Chief Field Headquarter in Warsaw District (signed Von Unruth) to Military Commander in General Government [at that time comprising military regions of Warsaw, Lublin, and Krakow].

May 20, 1941

The situation in the Jewish quarter is catastrophic. Dead bodies of those who collapsed from lack of strength are lying in the streets. Mortality, 80% undernourishment, has tripled since February. The only thing allotted to the Jews is 1½ pounds of bread a week. Potatoes, for which the Jewish Council has paid in advance of several million, have not been delivered. The large number of welfare agencies created by the Jewish council are in no position to arrest the frightful misery. The ghetto is growing into a social scandal, a breeder of illnesses and of the worst subhumanity. The treatment of the Jews in labor camps, where they are guarded solely by Poles, can only be described as bestial.

Monthly Deaths in 1941

	Number of Deaths			Daily Average			Monthly Rate in %		
	MEN	WOMEN	TOTAL	MEN	WOMEN	TOTAL	MEN	WOMEN	TOTAL
January	805	419	1,224	25.97	13.52	39.48	1.14	0.50	0.80
February	668	395	1,063	23.86	14.11	37.96	0.96	0.48	0.70
March	659	370	1,029	21.26	11.94	33.19	0.96	0.45	0.68
April	572	379	951	19.07	12.63	31.70	0.85	0.46	0.64
May	604	395	999	19.48	12.74	32.23	0.91	0.48	0.68
June	548	382	930	18.27	12.73	31.00	0.84	0.47	0.64
July	578	319	897	18.65	10.29	28.94	0.90	0.39	0.62
August	601	375	976	19.39	12.10	31.48	0.94	0.46	0.67
Sept.	439	326	765	14.63	10.87	25.50	0.69	0.41	0.53
October	364	280	644	11.74	9.03	20.77	0.55	0.33	0.42
November	519	409	928	17.30	13.63	30.93	0.74	0.45	0.57
December	599	432	1,031	19.32	13.94	33.26	0.85	0.47	0.63
Total, 1941	6,956	4,481	11,437	19.06	12.28	31.33	0.86	0.45	0.63

These comparative figures are based on the death register of Lodz for the year 1938 and on an estimate of 225,000 Jews in Lodz for the same year.

Monthly Rate in %

Jan.	Feb.	Mar.	April	May	Jun.	Jul.
0.10	0.08	0.09	0.09	0.09	0.09	0.07

Aug.	Sep.	Oct.	Nov.	Dec.	Jan.–Dec.	
0.09	0.08	0.11	0.08	0.10	0.09	

Deaths by Cause 1941 [monthly totals omitted]

	MEN	WOMEN	TOTAL	% OF TOTAL
Dysentery	155	89	244	2.13
Typhoid Fever	10	12	22	0.19
Spotted Fever	3	10	13	0.11
Diphtheria	3	5	8	0.07
Whooping Cough	3	2	5	0.04
Meningitis	2	2	4	0.03
Lung Tuberculosis	1,725	827	2,552	22.31
Other Tuberculosis	107	106	213	1.86
Other Lung Diseases	416	190	606	5.30
Heart Disease	1,873	1,348	3,221	28.16
Diseases of Nervous System	205	175	380	3.32
Diseases of Digestive System	445	295	740	6.47
Food Poisoning	11	14	25	0.22
Cancer and Tumors	40	99	139	1.22
Diseases of Old Age	244	261	505	4.41
Starvation	1,342	792	2,134	18.65
Freezing	9	6	15	0.13
Gunshot Wounds	27	13	40	0.35
Other	336	235	571	4.99
	6,956	4,481	11,437	100.00

[sic]

Daily Order No. 59
by Higher SS and Police Leader in Army District
XX/Chief of the Order Police (signed Knofe),
June 27, 1941

1. Citations . . .

d. Citation by Mr. Government President in Hohensalza: "On May 19, 1941 the 18-year-old auxiliary policeman Eduard Schulz, Protective Police, Department Kutno, acted resolutely to frustrate the escape of 5 Jews from the ghetto. They ducked out in a drainage canal which was strongly secured by barbed wire and, without the alertness and determination of the guard, would have disappeared in the dense terrain. The pursuit was extended over a distance of more than 1500 yards with the result that the 5 Jews were shot to death.

"Because of the vigilance, resolution, and good shooting of auxiliary policeman Schulz, the great danger of a spread of spotted fever and other epidemics to the German population was removed. I express my appreciation to Schulz for this conduct and sense of duty."

I join in this citation.

QUESTIONS TO CONSIDER

1. What did Jewish leaders like Chaim Rumkowski and Ephraim Barasz believe would keep the Jews of the Lodz ghetto free from harm? Why?

2. What tactics were used to get the Jews out of the ghettos and to the concentration camps?

3. How were the residents of the ghettos isolated? What was the effect of their isolation?

Life in Lodz

BY DAWID SIERAKOWIAK

Dawid Sierakowiak, a Polish Jew, was born in Lodz in 1925. When war came in August, 1939, Sierakowiak began to keep a diary of what happened. This diary records Poland's defeat, the arrival of the Germans, the creation of the huge ghetto in Lodz, and the deprivations suffered by the ghetto's inhabitants. Lodz was the largest of the Polish ghettos with more than 200,000 people forced into this sealed urban work camp. Sierakowiak died from tuberculosis on August 8, 1943. His diary is one of the most poignant records of the nightmarish existence of the ghettos.

LODZ, NOVEMBER 7, 1939

And so it's happened. Today's Deutsche Lodscher *Zeitung* announces the annexation of Lodz to Wartheland[1] and, thus, to the Greater Reich. Of course, the appropriate orders have been issued, namely: Jews are not allowed to walk on Piotrkowska Street, since it's the main street; Jews and Poles are to yield always and everywhere to uniformed Germans; wearing four-

---

[1] Wartheland—the western part of Poland, annexed into the Reich.

cornered hats, uniforms, army coats, shiny buttons, and military belts is forbidden. Jewish bakeries are permitted to bake only bread. Jewish stores are to be marked *"Jüdisches Geschaft"*[2] next to a yellow Star of David inscribed with the word *"Jude"* [Jew]. It's a return to the yellow patches of the Middle Ages.

LODZ, NOVEMBER 8, 1939

Terrible things are going on in town. Jews are grabbed and ordered to report tomorrow to a designated area, to bring a shovel, food for 2 days, and 20 zlotys. What new idea is this? What kind of agony? Posters on street corners announce the **annexation**[3] of Lodz to the Reich. A Nazi Youth Party was formed in the city: marching, singing, parades—one wants to stay home to keep from seeing all of this.

A meeting of "The Jewish Elders of Lodz" with the authorities was called for tomorrow. We'll see what comes of it.

LODZ, NOVEMBER 9, 1939

The Germans came to school yesterday and ordered that its Polish-Hebrew sign be taken down and the library made orderly.

LODZ, NOVEMBER 11, 1939

It's quiet in town, though yesterday and today they arrested a lot of teachers, activists who fought for Polish independence (in 1918), policemen, etc. The daily *Dziennik Lodzki* is discontinued as of today. An order was issued that all signs must be written in German, correctly, since we are now part of the Reich! As of the 15th all Poles and Jews must give up their radios. We'll have no news after that. The Germans do whatever they want.

---

[2] *Jüdisches Geschaft*—German for "Jewish business."

[3] **annexation**—the act of incorporating one country or territory into another.

LODZ, WEDNESDAY, NOVEMBER 15, 1939

The synagogue was burned down. Barbaric methods for annihilating the world are being activated. They demanded 25 million zlotys in exchange for stopping the terror. The community didn't have it, so it didn't deliver. Something is wrong with the Germans. Since yesterday they've been engaged in terrible plunder, robbing wantonly, whatever they can: furniture, clothes, underwear, food. All Lodz German males, 18 to 45, are being **mobilized**[4] today for *selbstschutz* [German for self-defense]. Since the regular army is leaving, someone has to stay and guard the city. We'll get the brunt of it. It's worse dealing with one Lodz German than a whole regiment from Germany.

LODZ, THURSDAY, NOVEMBER 16, 1939

We're returning to the Middle Ages. The yellow star is again part of the Jew's garb. An order was issued today that all Jews, regardless of age or gender, must wear a 10-centimeter armband—of "Jewish-yellow" color—on the right arm, directly below the armpit. In addition, Jews are to observe a curfew from 5 P.M. to 8 A.M.

LODZ, DECEMBER 11, 1939

Father came home with the news that starting today at 6 P.M. Jews will be deported from Lodz. All the neighbors packed bags, bundles, etc., and we did also, but nothing happened, and everyone eventually went to bed.

LODZ, DECEMBER 12, 1939

I saw a frightful sight. A Jew was being hit with a huge pole by a German. The Jew kept bending lower and lower without turning around, so as not to be hit from the front.

---

[4] **mobilized**—organized for war.

A new order was issued today: The yellow patches are to be removed, and 10 cm. yellow Stars of David are to be worn on the right chest and on the right side of the back.

LODZ, DECEMBER 13, 1939

There was more fear and anxiety when Dadek Hamer came to tell us that Jews are being driven into the empty market halls in Nowo-Zarzewska Street, to be sent into the Lublin district.

This evening we heard that the Jewish community administration has announced that the Jews must leave Lodz. Apparently, during the next four days, anyone can leave for any destination, except the Reich, and after that mass deportations will begin. The community administration will give the poor 50 zl. each and has started sending them out as of today. There is terrible panic in town, everyone has lost his head, but knapsacks and bundles are being packed.

LODZ, DECEMBER 14, 1939

Mass arrests continue into the third day: thousands of teachers, doctors, engineers with families (babies included) are driven into the empty market halls and then to German prisons. The same happens to old activists, former legionnaires, even ordinary rich men. Quite often, groups of important people are dispatched to their death.

LODZ, MARCH 21, 1942

This evening there was suddenly news that another 15,000 are to be deported immediately, in groups of a thousand a day. Everyone is saying that now all the ghetto's inhabitants will go.

LODZ, APRIL 20, 1942

The ghetto is going crazy. Thousands of those at risk are struggling every which way to get jobs, mostly through influence. Meanwhile, the German commission started its work. All those examined by the commission get an **indelible**[5] letter stamped on their chests, a letter whose significance nobody knows.

LODZ, APRIL 23, 1942

Last night the police went through apartments. Those who have not reported to the commission and could offer no excuse had to give up their bread and food ration cards. Today there were round-ups in the streets. There's talk that soon the entire population of the ghetto will be stamped.

LODZ, MONDAY, JULY 14, 1942

It seems that last year Rumkowski said that he couldn't save everyone and, therefore, instead of having the entire population die a slow death, he would save the "top ten thousand."

LODZ, FRIDAY, SEPTEMBER 4

There is terrible panic. No work is being done anywhere. Everyone is trying to get jobs for those not working. Parents are trying everything possible to save their children. The registrar's office was sealed after the lists were completed. Now any attempt at falsifying birth certificates, registry books or other documents is for naught. Today in our office job assignments were given out in great haste, even though there is talk that they're meaningless, because there will be orders confining everyone indoors. That way medical teams can decide who is fit for work.

As an office worker, I was able, despite great difficulty, to get a job in the furniture factory for my mother. In spite of this, I'm terribly worried about her, because she is emaciated and weak. She's not sick though and has worked in the vegetable gardens on the outskirts of

---

[5] **indelible**—something that cannot be removed, washed away, or erased.

the ghetto all along, and she cooks, cleans and does laundry at home.

In the morning, children between 8 and 10 were registered at the school office for work, but at 12 o'clock it was announced that these registration lists would be void. At 2 o'clock our office was closed, and we were all told to go home until further notice. All factories, offices and agencies were closed, except for food supply, sanitation wagons, police, firemen and various guards. Panic is increasing by the minute.

At 4 o'clock Rumkowski and Warszawski, the head of many factories, spoke at 13 Lutomierska. They said: Sacrificing the children and the elderly is necessary, since nothing can be done to prevent it. Therefore, please do not hinder our effort to carry out this action of deporting them from here.

It's easy for them, since they're able to get the Germans to agree not to take the children of factory heads, firemen, police, doctors, instructors, bureaucrats, and the devil knows who else. All kinds of favoritism will also be set in motion, and the Germans will get entirely different people than the 25,000 they've demanded, people who are fit for work but who'll be sacrificed for the elderly and children with pull.

In the evening, my father's cousin came to us with her 3-year-old girl, trying to save her. We agreed they could stay and later took in her whole family as well, because they're afraid to stay home, in case they're taken as hostages for the child.

Later there was an air raid; a few bombs were dropped, producing sounds that were bliss for every Jew in the ghetto.

SATURDAY, SEPTEMBER 5
My saintly, beloved, worn-out, blessed MOTHER has fallen prey to the bloodthirsty Nazi beast!!!!

In the morning fright enveloped the town, as news spread that last night some children and elderly were taken from their homes and placed in empty hospitals, from which they'll be deported beginning Monday, at a rate of 3,000 a day.

After 2 P.M., vehicles with medical examiners, police, firemen and nurses drove into our street, and the raid began. The house across from us was surrounded and after an hour and a half three children were brought out. The cries, screams and struggles of the mothers and everybody else on our street was indescribable. The children's parents were completely frantic.

While all of this was going on, two doctors, two nurses, a few firemen and policemen quite unexpectedly came to our house. They had a list of the tenants in every apartment. The doctors, sour and angry, from Prague, began examining everyone very thoroughly, despite objections from the police and nurses. They fished out many "sick and unfit" people, as well as those they described as "reserve." My unlucky, dearest mother was among the latter, which is no consolation, since they were all taken together to the hospital at 34 Lagiewnicka.

Our neighbor, 70-year-old Mr. Miller, the uncle of the ghetto's chief doctor, was spared, and my healthy though exhausted mother took his place!! The doctor who examined her, an old geezer, looked and looked for some ailment, and when he was surprised he couldn't find any, said to his companion, in Czech, "Very weak, very weak." He wrote down those two wretched words, despite protests from the police and nurses present. These doctors apparently didn't know what they were doing, because they also took David Hammer, a 20-year-old who has never been sick in his life. Thanks to his cousin, who's an official, he was re-examined and released, and the two doctors were denounced to the

Chairman and not allowed to examine anyone else. But what good is this to me?

My mother fell into the trap, and I very much doubt anything will save her.

After my mother's examination and while she was frantically running around the house, begging the doctors to save her life, my father was eating soup. True, he was a bit bewildered and approached the police and the doctors, but he didn't run outside to beg people he knew in power to **intercede**[6] on her behalf. In short, he was glad to be rid of a wife with whom life was lately getting too hard, a fact which Mother had to struggle with. I swear on all that is holy that if I knew Mother would not be sent to her death, that she'd survive after all, I'd be very pleased with things the way they are.

My little, exhausted mother, who has suffered so much misfortune and whose life has been one long sacrifice for family and others, would probably not have been taken because of weakness had she not been robbed of food by my father and Nadzia. My poor mother, who always believed in God and accepted everything that came her way, kept her clarity of mind even now, in spite of her great agitation. With a certain resignation and a heart-rending logic, she spoke to us about her fate. She agreed when I said that she'd given her life by lending and giving away so much food, but she said it in such a way that I knew she had no regrets, for even though she loved life dearly, there were things to value greater than life itself—such as God and family. She kissed each one of us goodbye, took a bag with some bread and potatoes in it, because I forced her to, and left quickly to meet her terrible fate.

LODZ, SUNDAY, SEPTEMBER 6

Yesterday afternoon notices were posted that from 5 P.M. until further notice no one may leave his apartment

---

[6] **intercede**—ask a favor from one person for another.

without a pass from the police. Excepting, of course, these, those, the others, and so on! Apparently, there is going to be a serious raid. At night a great many people were taken in other neighborhoods, but ours was relatively quiet. So far, all this is being done without the Germans and without slaughter—the one thing everyone fears. But let it happen—if only Mother could be returned to me!

Tonight there was no air raid and little said about miracles coming to us from the outside.

The heat is still extraordinary. In spite of the ban, people are running around the streets, everyone seeking help in his adversity. Now there is talk that the Germans are accompanying the medical teams, and they are deciding who should go and who should stay. All children previously exempted have now been told to report to one hospital, and though Rumkowski insists that the children's registers are iron-clad, no one believes him. Even policemen, instructors and managers are despairing. The cries, mad screaming and wailing are now so common that not much attention is paid to them. Why should I be moved by some other mother's cries, when they've taken my own mother away? No revenge would be enough for this deed!

On Bazarna Street huge gallows have been erected to hang some people from Pabianice who ran away before it was cleared of Jews. The devil knows why they need these gallows.

People who are hiding children in attics, lavatories and other holes are losing their heads in despair. Our street, which is very near the hospital, is filled all day with the wails of passing funeral processions, which follow the wagons of victims.

In the evening my father was able to get to Mother. He said the hospital is real hell—everyone is in terrible condition, everything is confused. Mother, apparently, is changed beyond recognition, which narrows her slim chance for release.

At times I get such jitters and heart spasms that I think I'm going insane or entering delirium. In spite of this, I cannot stop thinking of Mother, and suddenly I find myself, as though I were split in two, inside her mind and body. The hour of her deportation is approaching with no rescue in sight.

It rained a bit this evening, with some thunder and lightning, which did not lessen our suffering any. Even a torrential rain could not renew a torn heart.

QUESTIONS TO CONSIDER

1. In November of 1939, Jews and Poles were forced to give up their radios. Why do you think this rule was enforced?

2. What does Sierakowiak mean when he says "... the Germans will get entirely different people than the 25,000 they've demanded..."?

3. What happened to Sierakowiak's family and their relations to one another as a result of conditions in the ghetto?

The Last Morning

BY BERNARD GOTFRYD

The ghettos were essentially staging grounds for the concentration camps. As the Germans built more camps to provide labor for war industries, more and more slave labor was needed. The Germans rounded up able-bodied men for deportation. Eventually the round-ups took in all the residents of the ghettos as the Germans initiated their policies of annihilating all Jews. Bernard Gotfryd was a Polish Jew, born in Radom in 1920. He labored in six concentration camps, but survived the ordeal. After the war he emigrated to the United States and became a successful photographer. "The Last Morning" is a story about the roundups in the Polish ghettos. It is from Anton, The Dove Fancier *(1990), a collection of Gotfryd's stories and vignettes.*

I very clearly remember the day I saw my mother for the last time. It was Sunday the sixteenth of August, 1942, a beautiful day with a clear blue sky and hardly a breeze. That morning she got up very early, earlier than usual, and quietly, so as not to wake us, she went out to the garden. I was already up. I watched her through the kitchen window. She sat down on the broken bench behind the lilac tree and cried. I always felt bad when I saw my mother cry, and this time it was even more painful.

My mother was going to be forty-four years old at the end of August. She never made a fuss over her birthday, as if it were her own secret, and so I never knew the exact date. She was of medium height, rather plump, with a most beautiful face. She had large brown eyes and long, dark brown hair sprinkled with gray, which she pulled back into a **chignon.**[1] She smiled at people when she spoke and looked them straight in the eye.

When she came in from the garden she walked over to me and caressed my face as she used to do some years before the war, when I was a little boy. Now I was in my teens. Then she went over to the kitchen stove and started a fire. The wood was damp, and the kitchen filled with smoke. There was no more firewood left; this was the last of the broken-down fence from around our garden. She stood next to the stove fanning the smoke and asked me to open the door and the windows to let the smoke escape. Her eyes were red and teary, but when she turned to face me she smiled.

Soon the rest of the family was up, and Mother served a **chicory**[2] brew with leftovers of sweet bread she had managed to bake some days earlier. There was even some margarine and jam, a great treat. We sat wherever we could, since the table was too small for the five of us. Because of limited table space my grandmother and my aunt ate their meals in their own room. None of us had much to say that morning. We just stared at one another as if to reaffirm our presence.

Suddenly my mother lifted her eyes and, looking at my father, asked him, "What are you thinking about?" My father, as if he had just wakened from a deep

---

[1] **chignon**—a bun worn at the nape of the neck.

[2] **chicory**—an herb, the root of which is used to flavor coffee.

sleep, answered, "I stopped thinking, it's better not to think." We looked at him oddly. How could anyone stop thinking?

My mother got up from the table and started to tidy up the room. Then she asked me to go up to the attic and find her small brown suitcase for her. I found the suitcase, and, alone in the attic, I hugged it many times before I brought it to her.

The tension in the house nearly paralyzed me. It was stifling. I left in a hurry and, running all the way, went to investigate the ghetto square. It was still early in the morning, and clusters of people were congregating at street corners, pointing up at the utility poles. During the night the light bulbs had been replaced by huge reflectors. The ghetto police were out in force, preventing people from gathering. I noticed a poster reminding all inhabitants of the ghetto to deliver every sick or infirm member of their families to the only ghetto hospital. **Noncompliance**[3] called for the death penalty.

My paternal grandmother was recovering from a stroke. She was able to walk with the help of a cane. I trembled at the thought of having to turn her in. The Nazis were preparing something devious. I knew the hospital wasn't big enough to absorb all the sick people in the ghetto.

My mother studied my face when I came back from the square. There was a frightened look in her eyes. She asked me what was happening out there, what people were saying, and I lied to her. I didn't mention the reflector bulbs, but I could tell that she knew what was coming.

She had her suitcase packed, and her neatly folded raincoat was laid out on the couch, as if she were going on an overnight trip the way she used to before the war. No one said much. We were communicating through

---

[3] **noncompliance**—not following instructions or rules.

our silence; our hearts were tense. My father took out the old family album and stood at the window, slowly turning the heavy pages. I looked over his shoulder and saw him examining his own wedding picture. He pulled it out of the album and put it inside his breast pocket. I pretended not to see.

My mother started preparing our lunch, and I helped her with the firewood. There was no more fence left, and somebody had just stolen our broken bench. I found an old tabletop that Father kept behind the house, covered with sheets of tar paper. It was dry and burned well. I didn't tell my mother where the wood had come from; I was afraid she might not like the idea of putting a good table to the fire.

It was past noon, and my mother was busy in the kitchen. She found some flour and potatoes she had managed to save and came up with a delicious soup, as well as potato pancakes sprinkled with fried onions. Was this to be our last meal together? I wondered.

Some friends and neighbors with scared expressions on their faces dropped in to confirm the rumors about the coming deportation and to say good-bye. The Zilber family came, and everybody cried. I couldn't bring myself to say good-bye to anybody; I feared that I would never see them again.

It was getting close to four o'clock in the afternoon when my grandmother, dressed in her best, came out of her room. She was ready, she said, if someone would escort her to the hospital. My brother and I volunteered. She insisted on walking alone, so we held her lightly by the arms in case she tripped. She walked erect, head high; from time to time she would look at one of us without saying a word. People passed us in bewilderment. They seemed like caged birds looking for an escape. An elderly man carrying a huge bundle on his shoulders stopped us and asked for the time. "Why do you need to know the time?" I inquired. He looked at me as if upset by my question and answered, "Soon it will be time for evening prayers, don't you know?" And he went on his way, talking to himself and balancing the awkward bundle on his shoulders.

When we reached the hospital gate my grandmother insisted we leave her there. She would continue alone. With a heavy heart I kissed her good-bye. She smiled and turned toward us, saying, "What does one say? Be well?" Then she disappeared behind the crumbling whitewashed gate of the hospital. I needed to cry but was ashamed to do so in front of my older brother. Determined to prove how tough I was, I held back my tears. We walked back in silence, each of us probably thinking the same thing.

I'll never forget coming back to the house after escorting Grandmother to the hospital. My mother was in the kitchen saying good-bye to one of her friends. I had never seen her cry as she was crying. When she saw us she fell upon us, and through her tears she begged us to go into hiding. She begged us to stay alive so that we could tell the world what had happened. Her friend was crying with her, and I felt my heart escaping.

A neighbor came in to tell us that the ghetto was surrounded by armed SS[4] men, and it was official that the deportation was about to begin. The ghetto police were on full alert, and it was impossible to get any information out of them.

My brother and I turned and ran out of the house. Without stopping we ran the entire length of the ghetto until, dripping with sweat, we arrived at the fence. On the other side of the fence was a Nazi officers' club; farther off in the middle of a field stood a stable. By now the Ukrainian guards with their rifles were inside the ghetto. We scaled the fence behind their backs and made it across to the other side. We entered the stable through

---

[4] SS—Nazis who served as Hitler's bodyguard and as a policing unit of the German army.

a side door. As far as I could tell, no one was there. The horses turned their heads and sized us up. My brother decided we should hide separately, so that if one of us was discovered, the other one would still have a chance. I climbed up on the rafters and onto a wooden platform wedged in between two massive beams. There was enough hay to cover myself with, and I stretched out on my stomach. Through the wide cracks between the boards of the platform I could scan the entire stable underneath me. I also found a crack in the wall that allowed me a wide view of the street across from the stable.

A mouse came out from under a pile of straw, stopped for a second, and ran back in. I lay there trying to make sense of every sound. As I turned on my side I felt something bulky inside my pocket. I reached for it and discovered a sandwich wrapped in brown paper. My mother must have put it there when my jacket was still hanging behind the kitchen door.

As I replaced the sandwich I heard the door open and saw a man enter. He walked to the other end of the stable and deposited a small parcel inside a crate. Then he started to tend to the horses while whistling an old Polish tune. He must be the caretaker, I thought. He appeared to be still young, even though I couldn't clearly see his face; he walked briskly and carried heavy bales of hay with ease. I feared the commotion he was causing might attract attention; he kept going in and out, filling the water bucket for the horses to drink. I was getting hungry. I was about to bite into the sandwich when on one of his trips he looked up at the spot where I was hiding. I froze. Could it be that he had heard me move? I couldn't imagine what had made him look up, and I broke out in a sweat. I held on to the sandwich but was too upset to eat it. Every time he opened the door it squeaked, and the spring attached to it caused it to shut with a loud bang. He spoke to the horses in Polish with a provincial accent and called each horse by its name. He lingered with some of them, slapped their backs or gently patted their necks. How I envied him. Why was he free while I had to hide?

I started to recall the events of the entire day. I realized I had run out of the house without saying good-bye to my parents. Seized with guilt, I started sobbing.

I must have fallen asleep. When I woke up I heard loud noises coming from behind the fence. I looked through the crack in the wall; it was dark outside. Suddenly a loud chorus of cries and screams rang out, intermingled with voices shouting commands in German. Rifle shots followed, and more voices calling out names pierced the darkness. The cries of little children made me shudder.

I imagined hearing the screaming of my four-year-old cousin, who was there with his mother; my aunt, her sister, with her two beautiful little daughters. They were all there, trapped, desperate, and helpless. I thought of our friend Mr. Gutman, who some years before had claimed that God was in exile. I wondered where he was and what he was saying now. I worried about my grandmother and what they were doing to her at the hospital. Frightened and burdened with my misgivings, I resolved to go on, not to give in.

I heard the squeak of the door and looked down to see the caretaker slipping out. He blocked the door with a rock to keep it open. The sounds coming in from the outside were getting louder; the horses became restless and started to neigh. Rifle shots were becoming more frequent and sounded much closer than before. All these noises went on for most of the night—it felt like an eternity.

I could picture my mother in that screaming, weeping crowd begging me to stay alive, and I could hear her crying for help. Was my father with her, I kept wondering, and where was my sister?

It was almost daybreak when the noises began to die down. The sun was rising; it looked like the beginning of a hot August day. Only occasional rifle shots could be heard, and a loud hum that sounded as if swarms of bees were flying overhead; it was the sound of thousands of feet shuffling against the pavement. Looking through the crack in the wall, I could see long columns of people being escorted by armed SS men with dogs on leashes. Most of the people carried knapsacks strapped to their backs; others carried in their arms what was left of their possessions. I focused on as many people as I could, hoping to recognize a face. I wanted to know if my mother was among them and kept straining my eyes until I couldn't see anymore. I wondered if my brother, at the other end of the stable, was able to see outside. As it was, we had no way to communicate.

I kept imagining the moving columns of people getting longer and wider until there was no more room for them to walk. As I pictured them they kept multiplying; soon they walked over one another like ants in huge anthills, and the SS men weren't able to control them any longer.

Suddenly I heard voices underneath me. Before I realized who was there I saw the caretaker climbing up toward my hiding place. I couldn't believe it. I stopped breathing. Two SS men wearing steel helmets and carrying rifles stood at the door watching the caretaker climb. He came close to the platform where I was lying and in a loud voice told me to get down. "They came to get you," he said. "I knew you were here hiding. You can't outsmart me." I was betrayed.

Next he walked right over to where my brother was hiding and called him out. The two of us took a terrible beating from the SS men before they escorted us back to the ghetto. The first thing I saw in the ghetto was a large horse-drawn cart on rubber wheels, loaded with dead, naked bodies. On one side, pressed against the boards, was my grandmother. She seemed to be looking straight at me.

No dictionary in the world could supply the words for what I saw next. My mother begged me to be a witness, however; all these years I've been talking and telling, and I'm not sure if anybody listens or understands me. I myself am not sure if I understand.

The following night my brother and I miraculously escaped the final deportation, only to be shipped off to the camps separately soon afterward. I never saw my mother again, nor was I ever able to find a picture of her. Whenever I want to remember her I close my eyes and think of that Sunday in August of 1942 when I saw her sitting in our ghetto garden, crying behind the lilac tree.

QUESTIONS TO CONSIDER

1. What do the family members do as they prepare for their deportation? What do their actions reveal about their personal qualities? about their relationships with each other?

2. Why do you think the caretaker of the stable leaves the narrator and his brother in their hiding places for so long?

3. What does this story tell you about the fate of families during the Holocaust?

from

All But My Life

BY GERDA WEISSMANN KLEIN

Gerda Weissmann was born into a Jewish family in Bielitz, Poland in 1939. In 1939, the German army occupied the town, and the Weissmanns were forced into a ghetto. In 1942, the family was rounded up and sent to various concentration camps. Weissmann's brother had already been taken away, and her father, mother, and Gerda were sent to different camps. Weissmann survived her ordeal and wrote a frank, personal account of growing up in such circumstances. The following excerpt from All But My Life *describes the roundup in the Bielitz ghetto. Arthur was Weissmann's brother; Abek was her boyfriend.*

A few days later, on May 8, I woke up with Papa and Mama kissing me and saying "Happy birthday." Mama pressed something into my hand. An orange! I hadn't seen one in almost three years.

"Where did you get it, Mama?" But Mama would not tell. She smiled with the old merry twinkle in her sad eyes. Mama had always loved surprises.

Papa and Mama wanted me to eat all of the orange, but finally they each accepted a section. Later I learned from the Kolländers that Mama had given a valuable ring to obtain the one orange. It was the last birthday gift I was ever to get from my parents.

Abek came and brought me a portrait of Arthur that he had painted from a photo. I was touched by the thought, and the likeness was excellent. I placed it on the table and for a while it gave the illusion that Arthur was with us. Abek also brought roses for my birthday. Roses in the ghetto.[1] How unreal they looked! Somehow they were not mine, but I was tremendously pleased. Ilse, Rita, and Ruth came too. Ilse brought me a pin, a little white dog pin. Ruth and Rita brought note paper. Mama had made oatmeal cookies that tasted just like nut macaroons. "The rations, Mama?" I asked, but she just smiled in her old carefree way. I remember it as a very happy day and I shall never forget it.

My guests departed. I stood alone on the wooden balcony in the dusk. All of a sudden I had an intense longing for my garden. I closed my eyes and almost felt its aroma—the cool white lilacs kissed by a May rain. . . . I wanted to run, run home. If I ran fast I could be there in half an hour. But my garden was as remote as paradise. "I am eighteen years old," I confided to the old wooden post, "eighteen today."

Shortly after my birthday a notice was posted that all able-bodied persons were to register for work, inasmuch as there was a critical shortage of labor. A notice followed proclaiming that those who failed to register would be sent to Auschwitz, described in the notice as a newly created concentration camp about twenty miles away.

Papa, Mama, and I registered. Papa was told that he would work in Sucha, where the Germans were fortifying the river. It was a two-hour train ride. Mama and I

---

[1] ghetto—separate area in a large city, in which the Jews were forced to live.

were to work in Wadowitz in a shop that sewed military garments, which was about the same distance away but in a different direction. There was a general feeling of newly found security. The wages of course would be ridiculously small, barely enough to cover the train fare. But we would be safe now, and might be able to stay in the Bielitz ghetto.

Papa got up at four every morning. He had to be at work before seven. I trembled when I thought that he would have to push a wheelbarrow and work up to his knees in water. I ran home to our room every evening after work, grateful that he would be there for the all-too-short night. When Mama and I came home from work a little after eight, Papa was usually going to bed.

After a week or so Mama was not needed at the shop; for a while they had enough help. It was good that Mama did not have to go; she could have supper ready for us and keep our room in order. I enjoyed going to the shop, even though we had to assemble and march out of the ghetto under guard, and be counted like cattle at departure and arrival. The train ride was a pleasant break in the monotony. I loved seeing the forests we passed, the mountains in the distance, the meadows strewn with flowers. But best of all I liked to open the train window and shout at the top of my voice. The clatter of the wheels would drown my voice. To shout or sing was a luxury I hadn't enjoyed in a long, long time. There always were people close by, old people, sick people. On the train I could sing off key to my heart's content. . . .

One Friday we had to work longer than usual at the shop. It was quite dark as the train puffed through the sleepy landscape. We were not to work Saturday and Sunday and the two free days stretched ahead enticingly. I was in a gay mood, and gave the other girls imitations of people in the shop. I was quite good at it and the girls roared with laughter. The train stopped at a deserted little station. As Ilse and I stood at the open window we heard footsteps on the short platform. Then we heard voices and we saw two young men pass by. One of them said, "Today it's Andrichau, on Monday Bielitz." Ilse and I looked at each other. Was it? I felt a little nudging pain under my heart. We did not speak for the rest of the trip.

At home Papa was still up despite the lateness of the hour. He and Mama were both waiting for me. When I finished eating my supper, Papa motioned me to sit on his bed.

"What is it, Papa?" I asked, unable to bear the silence any longer. He stroked my hair but did not answer. Fear gripped me! Had they heard something too? When Papa said nothing I kissed him good night. He held me longer, much longer than usual. So did Mama.

I lay still in my bed, but sleep would not come. I was terribly afraid. And when finally I fell asleep I had horrible dreams. Toward morning I woke and saw Mama and Papa packing an old knapsack. I sat up in bed, demanding an explanation. For a moment there was silence; then Papa sat down on my bed and told me that in the morning—Saturday—he had to go to Sucha, where he worked. A camp was being formed there. On Monday Mama and I were to be moved to Wadowitz. Bielitz, our home town, would then be *Judenrein*—clear of Jews. Now I remembered what I had overheard at the little station. I wanted to shout, to cry out, to fight, but Papa's and Mama's strength kept me silent. How composed they were, packing and talking so casually!

We got word that Papa and the other men were to leave on Sunday, a day later than scheduled. A strange silence fell over the ghetto. I went downstairs to play with the little twins. I could not stand seeing Papa and Mama, yet I ran back every few minutes to be with them. Abek came. He and Papa embraced.

After supper, pretending to sleep, I listened to Papa and Mama talking. They talked both of the good life they had together and of what was to come—how the war would end soon, how Arthur would come back, and how he would have matured: "It is good for a man to have been away for a while," Papa commented. Presently, they discussed me: how much of life I had missed because of the war. "We will make it up to her," Mama said. "She shall have the prettiest dresses, dancing, and everything a young girl should have."

They talked about their parents, about the first years of their marriage, about waiting through the First World War . . . their reunion . . . when Arthur was born. Listening, I wanted to cry out—to reassure, to be reassured—but I bit my pillow in pain and kept silent.

And so they talked on through the night, animated and happy. They faced what the morning would bring with the only weapon they had—their love for each other. Love is great, love is the foundation of nobility, it conquers obstacles and is a deep well of truth and strength. After hearing my parents talk that night I began to understand the greatness of their love. Their courage ignited within me a spark that continued to glow through the years of misery and defeat. The memory of their love—my only legacy—sustained me in happy and unhappy times in Poland, Germany, Czechoslovakia, France, Switzerland, England. It is still part of me, here in America.

In the morning we did not talk about the train that was to leave a few hours hence. Silently we sat at the table. Then Papa picked up his Bible and started to read. Mama and I just sat looking at him. Then all of a sudden Papa looked up and asked Mama where my skiing shoes were.

"Why?" I asked, baffled.

"I want you to wear them tomorrow when you go to Wadowitz."

"But Papa, skiing shoes in June?"

He said steadily: "I want you to wear them tomorrow."

"Yes, Papa, I will," I said in a small voice.

I wonder why Papa insisted; how could he possibly have known? Those shoes played a vital part in saving my life. They were sturdy and strong, and when three years later they were taken off my frozen feet they were good still.

When it came time to leave, Papa and Mama embraced. Then Papa put his hands on my head in benediction, as he had done for Arthur. His hands trembled. He held me a while, then lifted my chin up and looked into my eyes. We were both weeping.

"My child," he managed. It was a question and a promise. I understood. I threw myself wildly into his embrace, clinging to him in desperation for the last time. I gave him my most sacred vow: "Yes, Papa." We had always understood each other, but never better than in that last hour.

And so we went to the station, across the meadow, taking the longer way, trying to be together as long as possible. A crowd was already assembled. Papa was asked for his identification. We went out onto the platform with him. The train would leave in a few minutes. People were saying their heartbreaking good-bys.

Papa entered the last car and went to the open platform at the rear to see us as long as possible. There he stood in his good gray suit, his only one, his shoulders sloping, his hair steel gray in the sun, on his breast the yellow star and black word.

There he stood, already beyond my reach, my father, the center of my life, just labeled J E W.

A shrill whistle blew through the peaceful afternoon. Like a puppet a conductor lifted a little red flag. Chug-chug-chug—puffs of smoke rose. The train began to creep away. Papa's eyes were fixed upon us. He did not move. He did not wave. He did not call farewell. Unseen hands were moving him farther and farther away from us.

We watched until the train was out of sight. I never saw my father again.

Only after several moments did I become conscious of the fact that Mama was with me. She took my hand like that of a baby and we started to walk toward the ghetto. I didn't once look at her. Only after a while did I realize that she too was weeping.

That night she fixed me something to eat and I ate to please her. She asked me to sleep with her in Papa's bed. I did so reluctantly. I was half asleep when I felt her arms around me, clinging to me in desperation. All my life I shall be sorry that I did not feel more tender that night. When Mama needed me most I wanted to be alone. I pulled away like a wounded animal that wants to lick its wounds in peace. Finally I fell asleep—on a pillow soaked with my mother's tears.

We rose early. While I put on my skiing boots Mama made me a cup of cocoa—the precious cocoa which she had saved for almost three years for a special occasion.

"Aren't you eating, Mama?" I asked.

"It's Monday," she answered. Mama had fasted every Monday for half a day since Arthur had left.

"But today," I said, "you should eat something."

"Today especially not," she answered from the window, holding the ivory-bound prayer book she had carried as a bride. She prayed and watched me—and I watched her. The chives were uprooted on the window sill. Yesterday we had taken out the few remaining jewels, sewed some into Papa's jacket, Mama's corset, my coat.

A shrill whistle blew through the ghetto. It was time to leave.

When we had made our way downstairs we saw the woman with the lovely complexion, Miss Pilzer, screaming and begging to be allowed to go with her mother. The dying old woman was thrown on a truck meant for the aged and ill. Here the SS[2] man kicked her and she screamed. He kicked her again.

On the same truck were Mr. Kolländer, the man with paralyzed legs, and the mother with her little girls. The twins were smiling; unaware of what was happening, they were busy catching the raindrops. An epileptic woman was put on the truck; her dog jumped after her. The SS man kicked him away, but the dog kept on trying to get in the truck. To our horror, the SS man pulled his gun and shot the dog. I looked toward Mama. I wanted to run to her. I wanted to be held by her—to be comforted. Now it was too late.

Leaving the invalids behind, we assembled in a field in a suburb of Bielitz called Lärchenfeld. Here we were left in the rain to wait. After about four hours the SS men finally came in a shiny black car, their high boots polished to perfection. A table was set up and covered with a cloth—a tablecloth in the rain!—and at that table they checked the lists of the people present.

We had all assembled.

Why? Why did we walk like meek sheep to the slaughterhouse? Why did we not fight back? What had we to lose? Nothing but our lives. Why did we not run away and hide? We might have had a chance to survive. Why did we walk deliberately and obediently into their clutches?

I know why. Because we had faith in humanity. Because we did not really think that human beings were capable of committing such crimes.

It cleared up and then it rained again. I was tired and hungry, hot and cold, and still we stood at attention, losing track of time.

---

[2] SS—Nazis who served as Hitler's bodyguard and as a policing unit of the German army.

Finally, certain trucks were loaded and driven off amid crying and screaming. Mama kept looking into my eyes. Her courage gave me strength. Those of us who remained were lined up in rows of four and ordered to march to the station. Instead of marching us across the meadow directly to the station, we were marched all around town. Oh God, I asked, I prayed, oh God, are they going to do to us what they did to Erika's mother? Will we dig our own grave? Oh God, no, no, NO! Don't let it happen—don't! I am afraid. I don't want to die. Don't hurt Mama. Don't—

I saw Bielitz, my dear childhood town. Here and there from behind a curtain a familiar face looked out. We kept on marching. People went marketing. Guards beat stragglers with rubber **truncheons.**[3] Oh God, I prayed, don't let it happen!

Someone pushed a baby carriage. Workmen were repairing a street. On the butcher shop they were painting a new sign. We were marching. A dry goods store was decorating its show window. We had bought the flowered fabric for my dress there, but it was not colorfast. Oh God, don't let it happen, don't, I prayed, don't! At the movie theater they were putting up a sign announcing a new feature—and we were marching.

I noticed Mama grow pale. She was gripping her suitcase tightly. I jerked it out of her hand.

"You hurt my hand," she said in a whisper.

Finally we approached the railroad station on the opposite side of town. Beyond the station were open meadows where the annual circus set up its tents. There we waited again.

From mouth to mouth the news traveled: "Merin!" Merin was here. The king of the Jews, as he was called, had arrived. His headquarters had been at Sosnowitz where there were the biggest Jewish congregation, the largest factories and shops in which Jews worked.

---

[3] **truncheon**—a stick cut and shaped for use as a weapon; club.

Customarily the Nazis established someone such as Merin as head of Jewish communities and gave him the job of liquidating them. It was said that Merin lived in luxury, that he had visited Goebbels, that he was the only Jew to own a car, that he was indescribably wealthy. I imagine these things were true. Certainly he was master of life and death.

I looked at him now. He was short, perhaps a bit over five feet, pale and thin; he had watery eyes, dull brown hair, and he was clad in a brown raincoat. He talked in a hoarse whisper. He pulled a bottle of schnapps[4] from his pocket, drank first and then handed it to the SS men about him. They drank after him. I saw it all and marveled. Yes, he was all right for them, he was their kind.

"I am glad you took the suitcase," Mama said very quietly. We were no longer standing at attention. "I would have fainted," she continued.

"Why didn't you throw it away?"

Her voice was without tone as she answered, "Arthur's picture is in it."

Merin was walking in our direction. Mama prompted me, "Go ask him if we are going to Wadowitz."

I asked him in Polish—it was known that his German was very poor.

He looked at me, his eyes without expression.

"Are you crazy?" was his hoarse reply.

Mama asked me what he had said, but I had no time to answer, for "All march down this way" came the command.

In our clenched fists we held our working cards from the shop, those sacred cards that we thought meant security. As we marched along in pairs we heard cries and screams ahead of us. Mama and I held hands tightly. A cane hit our hands.

---

[4] schnapps—strong liquor.

They unclasped. The cane pointed at me, a voice shouted, "How old?" My answer came, "Eighteen." The cane shoved me aside. Like a puppet I went. I knew Mama was marching on—in the opposite direction. I did not turn around. I could not. I knew she was looking at me as Papa had looked at us from the platform of the train. I knew that if I turned around we would have to run to each other—and that they would beat us or shoot us. We had to go on alone.

I was herded toward a group where my friends Ilse, Rita, and Ruth stood. Our parents were led to the other side of the meadow where a barbed wire enclosure had been set up. I did not see Mama, but we saw how earrings were torn out of ears, rings from fingers, and all thrown into a pail. I pictured Mama's wide wedding band with Papa's inscription in it among them, and I pictured the SS men digging greedily into the gold. Digging into people's love and pledges.

I saw a couple we knew. With their baby in their arms they walked up to the SS man, the judge of life and death. He told them to give the baby to those marching to the right, and motioned them to the group to the left. I saw the couple look at each other. Then I turned away, feeling the wide field revolving around me. When I looked again, sick and limp, I saw the couple embracing their baby—and walking slowly toward the right. . . .

We had assumed all along that we were going on a train, but now a truck came for us. I was the last one to enter it. Then I screamed, "I want to go to my mother!" and jumped down. Just then Merin passed. He looked at me, and with strength unsuspected in that little man, he picked me up and threw me back on the truck.

"You are too young to die," he said tonelessly.

I glared at him. "I hate you," I screamed. "I hate you!"

His eyes were without expression; there was a faint smile on his pale thin lips. It would have been easy for him to order me down and send me with my mother. Why did he not? Strange that the man who sent my mother to death had pushed me into the arms of life!

Someone fastened the canvas across the back of the truck and Merin walked away. Then above all the screams coming from behind the barbed wire I heard my mother. "Where to?" she called. I spread my arms and leaned out of the truck. I did not know the answer.

"Mama! Mama!" I called, as if the word could convey all I felt. Above all the confused, painful cries I heard Mama's voice again.

"Be strong!" And I heard it again like an echo: "Be strong." Those were my mother's last words to me.

As the trucks pulled away, the late afternoon sun came through the gray clouds for a moment. Its rays touched the roof of the church, glistening wet. The church bells were ringing. And then the sun disappeared.

Once more Bielitz was gray and dark, and as the truck rolled on, the city disappeared before my misty eyes.

QUESTIONS TO CONSIDER

1. What does Klein indicate is the most important thing she learned from her parents?

2. How did the skiing shoes help Klein?

3. According to Klein, why did she and the other women line up in the field and wait rather than run away and hide?

1980

BY ABRAHAM SUTZKEVER

*The poet Abraham Sutzkever was born in 1913 in Vilna, Lithuania.
When the Germans invaded Russia in 1941, they occupied Vilna.
More than 100,000 Jews were immediately shot, while the
remaining 20,000 were forced into ghettos. Sutzkever and his wife
survived, though their son was poisoned by the Germans. Much of
Sutzkever's poetry documents life in the ghetto: a life of constant
fear and hiding. Sutzkever was hidden by a Polish woman during a
period of roundups and his poem "1980" pays tribute to her.*

And when I go up as a pilgrim in winter, to recover
the place I was born, and the twin to self I am in my
  mind,
then I'll go in black snow as a pilgrim to find
the grave of my savior, Yanova.

She'll hear what I whisper, under my breath:
Thank you. You saved my tears from the flame.
Thank you. Children and grandchildren you rescued
  from death.
I planted a sapling (it doesn't suffice) in your name.

Time in its **gyre**[1] spins back down the flue
faster than nightmares of nooses can ride,
quicker than nails. And you, my savior, in your cellar
  you'll hide
me, ascending in dreams as a pilgrim to you.

You'll come from the yard in your slippers, crunching
  the snow
so I'll know. Again I'm there in the cellar, degraded
  and low,
you're bringing me milk and bread sliced thick at the
  edge.
You're making the sign of the cross. I'm making my
  pencil its pledge.

---

[1] **gyre**—a circular or spiral form or motion.

QUESTIONS TO CONSIDER

1. How does the speaker feel about Yanova? How can you tell?

2. What role did Yanova play not only in the speaker's life, but in the lives of others?

3. What do you think the last line of the poem means?

The
Concentration
Camps

from

A Generation
of Wrath

BY ELIO ROMANO

The first concentration camp was opened at Dachau shortly after Hitler came to power. The camp and its immediate successors were used to imprison Hitler's opponents in Germany. The Nazis eventually moved to interning all Jews, Gypsies, and homosexuals. These camps provided slave labor for various industries, and the ever-increasing number of Jews being interned helped fuel the expansion of Germany's war machine. In April, 1940, a town in East Upper Silesia in Poland was chosen for a new concentration camp, to be known as Auschwitz. Elio Romano was born in the town of Auschwitz in 1923. In 1940 he was forced to become a slave laborer by the Germans, eventually being sent to eleven different concentration camps. He survived and after the war wrote A Generation of Wrath: A Story of Embattlement, Survival, and Deliverance during the Holocaust of World War II. *The following selection describes the building of the camp at Auschwitz.*

A jail is a place where criminals and other temporary outcasts of society are locked up, I always thought. Being imprisoned was, of course, harsh punishment. In the town of Auschwitz, formerly the orderly and peaceful Oswiecim, the only people ever to land in the two jail cells located in the yard of the town hall, next to the police guardroom, were drunks who made a nuisance of themselves and insulted the town's **imperious**[1] police constable. Occasionally, socialist and communist **agitators**[2] during first-of-May[3] demonstrations had been temporarily "re-educated" there, before being sent away to bigger and more frightful installations in the capital. However, since the Germans had arrived, Auschwitz had neither drunks nor radicals. And so the jail block remained empty, until some twenty-five Jews filled its cells.

I was among those locked up and so was my mother. So were the others, either participants of the illegal escapade, parents or organizers. Yossel M was also among us. We never found out who put the finger on us, but betrayed we had been. That much we knew.

The minute the two German border guards took us back to their village post they boasted that they had known we were going to cross the border at a given point. All they had to do, they said, was trap us at the right time.

"You were sold out, you poor saps," the head of the border post, a middle-aged sergeant, told us after we were brought in by the patrol. Knowing the German invaders, we expected to be roughed up, beaten and interrogated, but nothing of the sort occurred. Instead, we were given food and hot tea with rum, as if we were guests instead of prisoners.

---

[1] **imperious**—haughty or arrogant.

[2] **agitator**—someone who stirs up public feelings for or against something, often for political reasons.

[3] **first-of-May**—In some parts of the world, labor parades and meetings are held on May Day (May 1).

Were these soldiers really Germans, I wondered? They were indeed, but not Wehrmacht **conscripts,**[4] only old border policemen, transferred from the Reich to do noncombatant duty along the new frontier. Old foxes they would be called by some, professionals who had wives and children back home and who apparently were glad to serve in an isolated post, away from the political Nazi Party goons who would see that the ideology of the "New Order" was scrupulously adhered to.

"You should be glad you were caught by us and not by the Gestapo," the sergeant said. We knew what he meant and appreciated his frankness. We hadn't eaten all day and the long march in the mountains froze our bones.

"What will happen to us?" I asked, after we had all been through a preliminary interrogation.

The sergeant shrugged. "Nothing, I suppose," he answered. "You'll go back home tomorrow. After all, you're still under age."

We were glad to hear that, but we knew that our adventure would cause **repercussions,**[5] once we got back to Auschwitz. The German authorities there wouldn't be as lenient as these old timers, veterans of Kaiser Wilhelm's[6] reign.

"Why couldn't you have let us cross the border?" I asked. "We only wanted to go to Palestine and we were told the Reich was glad to see us go."

"If it were up to me, I would have let you pass," the man answered, "but we received a tip about your intended crossing. You had no valid emigration permits, so we had to stop it. We do have martial law,[7] you know."

---

[4] **conscripts**—members of the military.

[5] **repercussion**—indirect influences or reactions from an event.

[6] Kaiser Wilhelm—last emperor of Germany, from 1888 until he abdicated the throne in 1918.

[7] martial law—rule by the army or militia with special military courts instead of the usual civil authorities. Martial law is declared during a time of trouble or war.

It was incredible. These Germans were of a different breed from those we had encountered until now. Had they, however, not been so duty conscious we would already have been in Slovakia. The next morning all eleven of us were given travel orders and train tickets to take us back to Auschwitz. We went all by ourselves.

Our adventure was rather short-lived. At home we had to put the armbands back on and keep a low profile. The meetings with Yossel M had been suspended, but we reported our experiences at a Jewish Council meeting, with our former mentor also present. Nobody could figure out who had given the scheme away. It didn't matter anyway. Youth emigration was dead and buried! But the belated after effects of our journey were soon to be felt.

Only three days after our return home we were called to the German police station and individually interrogated. This time we had to deal with professionals, but still they were only members of the *Schutzpolizei*, regular police constables and officers who went by the book. They, too, bore no grudges against Jews in particular, but had to prosecute a clear offense against their laws. In January 1940, the long arm of the Gestapo and the SS, about whom we had heard from previous Jewish refugees from Germany, had not yet reached Auschwitz.

I actually wondered why they had to grill us so much. They knew everything about our abortive escapade and the part Yossel M played in it. Anyway, I claimed ignorance. I just heard about the planned journey and simply joined in, I maintained. Of the organizers I knew nothing, I insisted. After all, I was only a youngster and still under age.

Again we were released and sent back home, but only temporarily. Within the next few days the German police and the Polish guard of the jail rounded up all the youngsters who had participated in the escape attempt, as well as all the parents they could find. I was thrown into a cell with the males and my mother joined the few females. Since we received no rations, our relatives were obliged to feed us. They were allowed to come once a day, during our fifteen minute walks in the yard, and give us our provisions. My mother and I were visited in the jail by my girl cousin, Hessa, who was about my age and our comforting angel then.

Since we never appeared before a court, we also didn't know how long we would be imprisoned. Yossel M reflected on past events in Europe.

"We have been fools all along," he told us. "In 1938, before the war started, Jabotinsky warned us about our fate, in the wake of Nazi expansionism, and urged us to leave Europe, but we didn't believe him. We were too complacent, too deeply rooted in our age-old habits to risk a change. Now, in 1940, our activities and movements are drastically curtailed and our resources limited. I am afraid that after our latest fiasco the Jewish Council will be unwilling to underwrite any further organized emigration or escapes. From now on every one of you is on his own. That is if we ever get out of this jail and the Germans don't ship us to one of their concentration camps."

Ever since the Nazi rise to power in Germany, in 1933, and from subsequent refugees, we all knew about the existence of such camps in Dachau, in Buchenwald . . . The people who were incarcerated there had been in jails first.

After seventeen days in the cell block we were released and allowed to go back home. That February the Germans weren't yet too preoccupied with Jews. To judge by their newspapers they still hoped Great Britain and France would opt for peace and approve the Reich's territorial gains. After all it was almost six months since the war began and yet all was quiet on the Western front. The game seemed to have been a wait-and-see proposition. It applied to us just as much as to the rest of the world.

Our economic situation however, had worsened. I went to work every day to supplement the family's income. The Maccabean[8] group had been disbanded, but I had been meeting my friends individually and often consulted with Julian and my cousin Jacob. The times weren't conducive to much cultural activity or social life. All we could do was talk about politics and survival.

In March the first SS man arrived in town. He was just a *Scharführer*, a corporal, but an arrogant thug whose sole purpose seemed to be to intimidate us. He arrived one morning in front of the office of the Jewish Council demanding one hundred workers for his command. Since the Council had other requirements to fill for the German Wehrmacht and police, the SS man got only fifty men that day. I was among them.

We were marched off to the former Polish barracks, across the river. The place had seen Jewish slave labor before, when we had had to remove all traces left by the previous occupants, the Polish artillery. This time, the SS man said, he would be in charge and we would be doing some "real work." We were going to be his work team, or *Kommando*, as he called it. Even then this martial term evoked in me a feeling of **ominous**[9] menace.

As soon as we reached the compound the SS man lined us up in columns of three abreast and had us stand at attention. It looked like some kind of army drill and we didn't know what to make of it. We didn't have to wait long for an explanation. With a horse whip in his hand to make him feel masterly, the *Scharführer* posted himself in front of us and started to give us a lecture.

---

[8] Maccabean—reference to Judas Maccabaeus, the leader of a successful Jewish revolt in 166 BC against Syrian rule of Palestine.

[9] **ominous**—unfavorable; threatening.

"Listen carefully, you pigheaded scum! I came here to teach you obedience and subservience. We Germans will make you pay dearly for slandering the Reich and our Fuehrer."

While he looked us over carefully, this conglomerate of shabbily dressed youngsters and middle-aged men, he continued to spill his venom. We were terror-stricken.

"You miserable gang of poor-Johns may not be the real culprits, but the American **plutocrats**[10] and their Jews are. They forced the war upon us. And so you *Schweinehunde* will suffer for their crimes. All of you are warmongers!"

I stood there petrified. What the man said was hideous and the most terrible slander the Nazis could use against us. Yet we didn't dare to contradict him.

"You see," the SS goon continued in triumph, "your silence proves that I am right. I have seen your crooked kind before, back home, in the concentration camp of Sachsenhausen. Mark that in your cowardly brains!"

So, that was it. The black plague had finally come to Auschwitz. If one SS man came, others were bound to follow. What sinister plans were they hatching?

I had no time to speculate further because the *Scharführer* made us do punishing exercises and push-ups.

"This will circulate your rotten blood," he laughed viciously. "After that you'll be fit for honest work."

Following the drill period we were assigned to work. All the buildings had to be emptied of furniture and all the rubble burned on an empty plot. We started with the first of some 20 one- and two-story brick buildings spread over the entire compound.

From that first day, the Jewish Council allocated higher pay for all the workers who went out on the barracks detail. It was a case of hardship, but many of our

---

[10] **plutocrats**—people who have power or influence because of wealth.

people needed the income, myself included. In about a month all the buildings had been cleared. In the meantime Polish masons and carpenters had been hired by the Germans and a few of the better-kept buildings were renovated. Also, strings of barbed-wire fences had been laid all around the compound and watchtowers built. There was no doubt in our minds that the former barracks would become some sort of prison camp. As time went on our work detail swelled to between two to three hundred men. At first, the SS man had us do the push-up ritual daily, but he soon got tired of it himself and relented. The workday became routine.

Some time in April a troop of about fifteen more SS men, headed by an officer named Höss, arrived in Auschwitz and took up quarters in one of the refurbished buildings. With them German "Aryan" concentration-camp prisoners in striped uniforms, some thirty men in all, also came. We found out that they were from Sachsenhausen, near Berlin. They, too, occupied one of the blocks, but behind barbed wire. Clean-up and restructuring work had then been going on in full swing. We realized with horror that the SS were building another one of their sordid camps, but this time on our own soil! Most ominous, however, was the disinfection process the Germans devised.

As a self-proclaimed superior race, the Germans always held the opinion that other peoples were not hygienic enough, according to their own standards, and therefore their dwellings must surely be infested by vermin. To make the old Polish buildings "habitable" they had to be disinfected. This was done by **hermetically**[11] sealing a building first, sticking mud into all roof crevices and plastering adhesive tape around door and window frames, and then fumigating the interior. The disinfecting agent was a crystalline chemical in tin cans

---

[11] **hermetically**—airtight.

which, when evaporating, had that cleansing effect. The used-up containers were discarded and, like all other rubbish, landed on a big dump which was periodically set on fire. I once looked at one of the empty cans. It was a sinister, deathbearing vessel and its chemical contents was called Zyklon-B.[12] Had the can not been so bulky, I would have taken it home with me, as I had been pocketing labels which came with various shipments we had to unpack and handle before the items were delivered to their designated places. In all instances the slips said, *Konzentrationslager Auschwitz,* making them valid souvenirs for the collector I was. The tin can was more than that. As I held it in my hands, an awesome, inexplicable premonition struck me that this poisonous chemical could also be used to "disinfect" people. The thought was so morbid that I became distressed and threw the **macabre**[13] item on to the burning fire.

That day the camp's loudspeakers blared martial music. It was Saturday, the 20th of April 1940. Hitler's birthday.

Little by little the new concentration camp took shape. The compound was a beehive of activity. Several hundred Jews and Poles worked there daily under the supervision of German civilians, while the German prisoners from Sachsenhausen were preparing quarters for more inmates and the SS guards walked around the new installation like peacocks, drinking mineral water at all conceivable hours. At the time, I thought this was some sort of ritual which I could never comprehend. Only later, a friendly German supervisor offered a plausible explanation. Mineral water purified body and mind, according to Himmler,[14] and his SS men were ordered to drink it.

---

[12] Zyklon-B—a cyanide-based gas manufactured by a pest control company during World War II.

[13] **macabre**—gruesome; horrible; ghastly.

[14] Himmler, Heinrich—director of Nazi propaganda from 1926-1930. He eventually became head of all German police forces.

In May, a transport of some forty Polish prisoners arrived from Dachau. They were to become the so-called *Stammhäftlinge*, the basic inmates of the Auschwitz Concentration Camp. Although they were quartered in a compound behind barbed wire, I had a chance to talk to them. Some of them were Jews from Warsaw. They had been taken to Dachau not as Jews, but as part of a raid on Polish **intelligentsia**.[15] One of them told me that they were to become the camp's administrators, cooks and book-keepers, with the German prisoners from Sachsenhausen, a mixed conglomerate of men, the camp's future "Capos."

"Capos?!" I asked.

"The sons-of-bitches are our supervisors," the gentle-looking Jewish prisoner answered. "The Germans plan to imprison thousands of people here. I hope you won't be one of them."

I was frightened out of my wits. "What can I do for you?" I asked the prisoner. "Do you have relatives?"

"We are allowed to write home, once a month," he answered, "but the food here is poor."

While nobody was looking, I slipped the sandwich I had brought for lunch through the barbed wire. He took it furtively and left. In the days to follow, I could see some of my comrades from the Jewish work detail do the same. We supported the prisoners as much as we could. Bread was the one commodity we could still spare. After all it was heartbreaking to see fellow human beings caged in behind barbed wire. Life in such a spine-chilling camp was anything but recreation, we knew. It was indeed a hell on earth.

Our work detail in the camp lasted till some time in June, after which no Jew from the town of Auschwitz

---

[15] **intelligentsia**—persons representing the superior intelligence or enlightened opinion of a country; the intellectuals.

was allowed anywhere near the perimeter of the concentration camp. Occasionally, columns of prisoners marched through town, on the way to their places of work. I saw hundreds of them, flanked by SS guards, while those with armbands designating them as Capos headed the various details.

It was truly a dispiriting sight.

QUESTIONS TO CONSIDER

1. How were the officers who caught the narrator during his botched escape attempt different from the SS officers who were in command of setting up the camp?

2. Which images in this account are most memorable and haunting for you?

3. The narrator's sister asks, "What is a concentration camp?" Based on this selection, how would you answer her question?

The Wannsee Conference

BY MARTIN GILBERT

Throughout 1940 the Nazi leadership struggled with what they termed the "Jewish Problem." The maintenance of the ghettos and work camps was a logistical nightmare. As the German army prepared for the invasion of Russia in 1941, the SS created a series of special killing squads, the einsatzgruppen. These groups were given orders to shoot captured Russian Jews. The creation of these killing squads marked the beginning of the Nazi's purposeful plan to annihilate the Jews. The success of the SS groups led to the creation of police battalions that carried on the same work in the occupied territories in eastern Europe. Throughout 1941, large numbers of western Jews were being deported to the ghettos of the east. The overcrowding led to various experiments with killing masses of people. In September, at Auschwitz, nine hundred people were gassed to death in a bunker and gassing in mobile vans began at Chelmno shortly thereafter. Early in 1942, Reinhard Heydrich, Hitler's deputy in charge of what was termed the "Final Solution to the Jewish problem," convened a conference at Wannsee, near Berlin, to implement a deliberate plan of genocide.

The Wannsee Conference took place on 20 January 1942. The notes which were taken of its deliberations make no reference to the gassings which had taken place at Chelmno throughout the previous forty-four days; a period during which more than forty thousand Jews and Gypsies had been murdered. According to the notes of the Conference, Heydrich[1] began telling the assembled senior civil servants of his appointment "as **Plenipotentiary**[2] for the Preparation of the Final Solution of the European Jewish Question." As a result of this appointment, he told them, it was his aim "to achieve clarity in essential matters." Heydrich went on to tell the Conference that Goering had asked to see "a draft project" of organizational, factual and material "essentials" in consideration of this "final solution."[3] Such a draft, he added, would require "prior joint consultation" of all the ministries involved "in view of the need for parallel procedure."

The struggle waged against the Jews "so far," said Heydrich, had first involved the expulsion of the Jews "from various spheres of life of the German people" and then the expulsion of the Jews "from the living space of the German people." Now, following "pertinent prior approval of the Führer," the "evacuation of the Jews to the East" had emerged "in place of emigration" as a "further possible solution." But both emigration and evacuation, he pointed out, were to be considered "merely as a measure of expediency," from which experience could be gained which would be of importance "in view of the approaching final solution of the Jewish question."

Heydrich then explained that this "final solution" concerned, not only those Jews who were already under

---

[1] Heydrich—head of the Nazi security police until his assassination in 1942.

[2] **plenipotentiary**—having or giving full power or authority.

[3] final solution—the slaughter of the Jews, commanded by Adolf Hitler. The mass killing now has the name genocide in the international community.

German rule, but "some eleven million Jews" throughout Europe. He then gave the meeting a list of the numbers involved, including 330,000 Jews in as yet unconquered Britain. All the Jews in the neutral countries of Europe were also listed: 55,500 in European Turkey, 18,000 in Switzerland, 10,000 Jews in Spain, 8,000 Jews in Sweden, 4,000 Jews in the Irish Republic and 3,000 in Portugal.

The figures presented by Heydrich included 34,000 for Lithuania. The other 200,000 Jews of pre-war Lithuania had, though he did not say so, been murdered between July and November 1941 by Einsatzgruppe A, their numbers meticulously listed town by town and village by village in Colonel Jaeger's report of 1 December 1941.

The largest number of Jews listed by Heydrich were those in the Ukraine: his figure was 2,994,684. The second largest was for the General Government, 2,284,000. The third largest was for Germany's ally, Hungary, 742,800, a figure which included the Jews in Ruthenia, Transylvania and those areas of Czechoslovakia annexed by Hungary in 1938 and 1939. The fourth highest figure was for unoccupied France, 700,000, a figure which included the Sephardi Jews in France's North African possessions, Morocco, Algeria and Tunisia. Next largest in the list was White Russia, 446,484, followed by the 400,000 Jews of the Bialystok region.

Hungary was Germany's ally. Jews living in five other countries which were allied to Germany were also listed: 342,000 in Rumania, 88,000 in Slovakia, 58,000 in Italy, including Sardinia, 40,000 in Croatia and 2,300 in Finland. The smallest number given was the 200 Jews of Italian-occupied Albania. Estonia was listed as "without Jews." This was true. Of Estonia's 2,000 Jews in June 1941, half had fled to safety inside the Soviet Union, while half had already been killed by the Einsatzkommando.

The senior officials present at the Wannsee Conference were from the Ministry for the Occupied Eastern Territories, the Ministry of the Interior, the Justice Ministry, the Foreign Office, the General Government of Poland, the Chancellery, and the Race and Resettlement Office. Also present was the Plenipotentiary for the Four Year Plan, responsible for disposing of Jewish property. All were asked by Heydrich to cooperate "in the implementation of the solution." His remarks continued:

> In the course of the final solution, the Jews should be brought under appropriate direction in a suitable manner to the East for labor utilization. Separated by sex, the Jews capable of work will be led into these areas in large labor columns to build roads, whereby doubtless a large part will fall away through natural reduction.
>
> The inevitable final remainder which doubtless constitutes the toughest element will have to be dealt with appropriately, since it represents a natural selection which upon liberation is to be regarded as a germ cell of a new Jewish development.

Heydrich then explained the European aspect of the plan:

> In the course of the practical implementation of the final solution, Europe will be combed from West to East. If only because of the apartment shortage and other socio-political necessities, the Reich area—including the **Protectorate**[4] of Bohemia and Moravia—will have to be placed ahead of the line.
>
> For the moment, the evacuated Jews will be brought bit by bit to so-called transit ghettos from where they will be transported farther to the east.

---

[4] **protectorate**—a weak country under the protection and partial control of a strong country.

It was intended, according to the statistics presented to the Wannsee Conference, that a total of eleven million European Jews should "fall away," including those in the neutral and unconquered countries. The Conference discussed the various problems involved. "In Slovakia and Croatia," they were told, "the situation is no longer all that difficult, since the essential key questions there have already been resolved." As for Hungary, "it will be necessary before long," Heydrich told the Conference, "to impose upon the Hungarian government an adviser on Jewish questions." Rumania posed a problem, as "even today a Jew in Rumania can buy for cash appropriate documents officially certifying him in a foreign nationality." Speaking of the occupied and unoccupied zones of France, however, Heydrich commented that there "the seizure of the Jews for evacuation should in all probability proceed without major difficulty."

The representative of the General Government, Dr. Joseph Buhler, stated that his administration "would welcome the start of the final solution in its territory, since the transport problem was no overriding factor there and the course of the action would not be hindered by considerations of work utilization." Buhler added:

> Jews should be removed from the domain of the General Government as fast as possible, because it is precisely here that the Jew constitutes a substantial danger as carrier of epidemics and also because his continued black market[5] activities create constant disorder in the economic structure of the country. Moreover, the majority of the two and a half million Jews involved were not capable of work.

---

[5] black market—the selling of goods at illegal prices or in illegal quantities.

Buhler had, he said, "only one favor to ask," and that was "that the Jewish question in this territory be solved as rapidly as possible."

The meeting was drawing to its end. "Finally," the official notes recorded, "there was a discussion of the various types of solution possibilities."

What these "possibilities" were, the notes of the Conference do not record.

"I remember," Adolf Eichmann[6] later recalled, "that at the end of this Wannsee Conference, Heydrich, Muller and myself sat very cozily near the stove and then I saw Heydrich smoke for the first time, and I thought to myself, 'Heydrich smoking today': I'd never seen him do that. 'He is drinking brandy': I hadn't seen him do that for years." After the Conference, Eichmann recalled, "we all sat together like comrades. Not to talk shop, but to rest after long hours of effort."

The "long hours of effort" were over. As Heydrich knew, the time was right for the deportation and destruction of millions of people. From many parts of Europe, there was evidence that only one more step had to be taken, and could be taken: the step already tried in the villages around Chelmno: the uprooting of whole communities, and their total disappearance. Few, if any, would care to inquire what had become of them. In hidden camps, a small band of sadists could then destroy them.

What had hitherto been tentative, fragmentary and **spasmodic**[7] was to become formal, comprehensive and efficient. The technical services such as the railways, the bureaucracy and the diplomats would work in harmony, towards a single goal. Local populations would

---

[6] Adolf Eichmann—member of the Nazi secret police beginning in 1934, Eichmann eventually was in charge of overseeing the "final solution to the Jewish problem."

[7] **spasmodic**—occurring very irregularly; intermittent.

be **cajoled**[8] or coerced into passivity. Some would even cooperate: that had been made clear already. On January 9 the Polish underground in Warsaw had warned the Polish Government in Exile of "a blind and cruel anti-Semitism" among the Polish population, itself the victim of Nazi terror.

By the end of January 1942, the Germans needed only to establish the apparatus of total destruction: death camps in remote areas, rolling stock, timetables, confiscation patterns, deportation schedules, and camps; and then to rely upon the tacit, unspoken, unrecorded **connivance**[9] of thousands of people: administrators and bureaucrats who would do their duty, organize round-ups, supervise detention centers, coordinate schedules, and send local Jews on their way to a distant "unknown destination," to "work camps" in "Poland," to "resettlement" in "the East."

The officials present at the Wannsee Conference had agreed with Heydrich's suggestion that the "final solution" should be carried out in coordination with Heydrich's own "department head," Adolf Eichmann. The result of this decision was that Eichmann's representatives now travelled to all the friendly European capitals. Although they were attached to the German Embassies, they received their instructions direct from Eichmann's section in Berlin and reported back to Eichmann, by telegram, as each deportation was planned and carried out.

In addition to the technical arrangements involving thousands of trains and tens of thousands of miles, a complex system of **subterfuge**[10] had to be created, whereby the idea of "resettlement" could be made to appear a tolerable one.

---

[8] **cajole**—to deceive with soothing words or false promises.

[9] **connivance**—to pretend not to know about or to fail to take action against wrongdoing.

[10] **subterfuge**—trick or excuse used to escape something unpleasant.

All this was done by Eichmann's section, whose representatives were soon active in France, Belgium, Holland, Luxembourg, Norway, Rumania, Greece, Bulgaria, Hungary and Slovakia. Regular meetings were held in Berlin to coordinate the complex yet essential aspect of the impending deportations: the despatch of full trains and the return of empty trains. In a document dated 13 January 1943, and signed by Dr. Jacobi of the General Management, Railway Directorate East, in Berlin, one sees the amount of work, and the number of people, involved in these deportation plans. The document took the form of a "telegraphic letter" addressed to the General Directorate of East Railways in Cracow; the Prague Group of Railways; the General Traffic Directorate, Warsaw; the Traffic Directorate, Minsk; and the Railway Directorates in fourteen cities, including Breslau, Dresden, Königsberg, Linz, Mainz and Vienna. Copies were also sent to the General Management, Directorate, South, in Munich, and to the General Management, Directorate West, in Essen: a total distribution of twenty copies. The subject was: "Special trains for resettlers" during the thirty-nine days from 20 January to 28 February 1943.

By the time of this railway telegram, sent a year after Wannsee, the transport aspects of the "final solution" were well tested, and well arranged. For anyone whose cooperation was needed, but who might be reluctant to cooperate, the full rigors of Nazi terror were readily available: perfected even at the time of Wannsee by nine years of Nazi rule and practice.

On January 30, nine years after coming to power in Germany, and only ten days after the Conference on the shore of Wannsee, Hitler spoke at the Sports Palace in Berlin of his confidence in victory. He also spoke of the Jews, telling his listeners, as reported by the Allied[11]

---

[11] Allied—describing the countries that fought against Germany, Italy, and Japan in World War II.

monitoring service on the following day: "They are our old enemy as it is, they have experienced at our hands an upsetting of their ideas, and they rightfully hate us, just as much as we hate them." The Germans, Hitler added, were "well aware" that the war could only end when the Jews had been "uprooted from Europe," or when "they disappear." Hitler then declared, as recorded by the Allied monitoring service:

> . . . the war will not end as the Jews imagine it will, namely with the uprooting of the Aryans, but the result of this war will be the complete **annihilation**[12] of the Jews.
>
> Now for the first time they will not bleed other people to death, but for the first time the old Jewish law of an eye for an eye, a tooth for a tooth, will be applied.
>
> And—world Jewry may as well know this— the further these battles [of the war] spread, the more anti-Semitism will spread. It will find nourishment in every prison camp and in every family when it discovers the ultimate reason for the sacrifices it has to make. And the hour will come when the most evil universal enemy of all time will be finished, at least for a thousand years.

Such was Hitler's message, as received in London and Washington: the war would end with "the complete annihilation of the Jews."

Even as Hitler spoke, new death camps were being prepared. Three of the sites chosen were remote villages on the former German-Polish border, just to the west of the River Bug. Although remote, each site was on a railway line linking it with hundreds of towns and villages whose Jewish communities were now trapped and starving. The first site, at Belzec, had been a labor camp

---

[12] **annihilation**—destruction.

in 1940: the railway there linked it with the whole of Galicia, from Cracow in the west to Lvov in the east, and beyond; and with the whole of the Lublin district. The second site, at Treblinka, also the site of an existing labor camp, was linked by rail, through both Malkinia junction, and Siedlce, with Warsaw and the Warsaw region. The third site, at Sobibor, a woodland halt where Jewish prisoners-of-war had been murdered in 1940, linked by rail to many large Jewish communities, among them Wlodawa and Chelm.

Although a tiny handful of Jews, like Michael Podklebnik and Yakov Grojanowski, might be chosen in these camps as a small labor force to dispose of the corpses, or to sort out the clothes of the victims, most of the deportees were gassed[13] within hours of their arrival, husbands with their wives, mothers with their children, the old, the sick, the infirm, pregnant women, babies; no exceptions were made and no mercy was shown.

Later, camps were to be set up at which as many as half of the deportees were "selected" for forced labor, but at Chelmno, Belzec, Sobibor and Treblinka no such "selections" were made. In these four camps, between the early months of 1942 and the first months of 1943, many hundreds of Jewish communities were to be wiped out in their entirety: more than fifty communities at Chelmno alone. Yet within a few months Chelmno was to prove the second smallest of the four death camps; a camp at which, nevertheless, at least 360,000 Jews were killed within a year.

A fifth camp was also set up in the spring of 1942, an extension of an existing camp, Auschwitz. Situated across the railway line from Auschwitz Main Camp, where Polish prisoners suffered cruel torments, the

---

[13] gassed—forced into a confined, sealed area into which poisoned gas was released in order to induce death.

new camp was in a birch wood, known in German as Birkenau.

At the railway yard near Auschwitz station, a selection was to be made of each incoming train, and as many as half those brought to the camp were to be "selected," not for gassing, but for forced labor. The labor was, first, in the camp itself, and subsequently in the surrounding factories of East Upper Silesia: coal mines, synthetic coal and rubber factories, and other military and industrial enterprises. From each train, however, of a thousand deportees, at least five hundred were to be gassed within a few hours of their arrival: all old people, all those who were sick, all cripples and all small children. The gassings took place, at first, in a gas-chamber in Auschwitz Main Camp, or in a specially constructed gas-chamber in the birch wood.

Auschwitz was not a remote village in eastern Poland, but a large town at a main railway junction, in a region annexed to the German Reich. The railway was part of a main line, with direct links to every capital of Europe: to the Old Reich, to Holland, France and Belgium, to Italy, and to the Polish railway network.

Fewer Jews were to be killed at Auschwitz-Birkenau than at the four death camps combined, but far more Jews were to survive Auschwitz-Birkenau, having been "selected" for slave labor, than were to survive the four death camps. Indeed, from Belzec there were to be no more than two survivors, from Chelmno only three, from Treblinka less than forty, and from Sobibor a total of sixty-four; while from Auschwitz-Birkenau, several thousand Jews were to survive. But in February 1942 all this was in the future: the special gas-chambers in these camps were still under construction, except at Chelmno, whose gas-vans had been working without interruption since 8 December 1941. By the time of the Wannsee Conference, three special gas-vans were in operation at

Chelmno. "At the beginning, Jews were brought to Chelmno daily," recalled Andrzej Miszczak, a resident of Chelmno village. "The gendarmes used to say, 'Ein Tag—ein tausend,' 'One day—one thousand.'"

QUESTIONS TO CONSIDER

1. What plans were made at the conference to deal with the "Jewish problem"? What was the scope of this plan?

2. Hitler believed that World War II would end with the annihilation of the Jews. Why did he make this claim?

3. What were Jews told about where they were going in order to lure them to these death camps?

One Year in Treblinka

BY JANKIEL WIERNIK

Chelmno was the first concentration camp where the Germans experimented with mass killings, in December 1941. In the wake of the conference at Wannsee, three more death camps were created, at Belzec, Sobibor, and Treblinka. In 1942, Treblinka began to devote itself solely to gassing of its prisoners. Jankiel Wiernik (1890–1972) was a Polish Jew. In 1942, he was sent to Treblinka, where he was spared from the gas chambers because of his skill as a carpenter. He escaped in August 1943 during an uprising and was able to join the Jewish underground. At the urgings of his comrades, Wiernik wrote an account of Treblinka, which was smuggled to the West in 1944 and was one of the first accounts of genocide to find a wide audience. Eight hundred forty thousand people were gassed at Treblinka; there were fewer than forty people who survived the camp.

It happened in Warsaw on August 23, 1942, at the time of the ghetto blockade. I had been visiting my neighbors and was never able to return to my own home. We heard the crack of rifle fire from every direction, but had no inkling of the whole truth. Our terror was intensified by the entry of German Scharführers[1] and of Ukrainian militiamen who shouted in menacing tones: "Everybody out!"

In the street one of the leaders arranged the people in ranks, without any distinction as to age or sex, performing his task with glee, a satisfied smile on his face. Agile and quick of movement, he was here, there and everywhere. He looked us over appraisingly, his eyes darting up and down the ranks. With a sadistic sneer he contemplated the great accomplishment of his mighty Fatherland which, at one stroke, would chop off the head of the loathsome serpent.

I looked at him. He was the vilest of them all. Human life meant nothing to him, and to inflict death and untold torture was his supreme delight. Because of his "heroic deeds," he subsequently was promoted to the rank of Untersturmführer.[2] His name was Franz. He had a dog named Barry, about which I shall speak later.

I was standing on line directly opposite the house on Wolynska Street where I lived. From there, we were taken to Zamenhof Street. The Ukrainians divided our possessions among themselves before our very eyes. They fought over our things, opened up all bundles and assorted their contents.

Despite the large number of people in the street, a dead silence hung like a **pall**[3] over the crowd. We had been seized with mute despair—or was it **resignation?**[4] And still we did not know the whole truth. They photographed us as if we were prehistoric animals. Part of the crowd seemed pleased, and I myself hoped to be

---

[1] Scharführer—staff sergeant.

[2] Untersturmführer—lieutenant.

[3] **pall**—something that produces an effect of gloom.

[4] **resignation**—a state of having given up.

able to return home, thinking that we were merely being put through some identification procedure.

At a word of command we got under way. And then, to our dismay, we came face to face with stark reality. There were railroad cars, empty railroad cars, waiting to receive us. It was a bright, hot summer day. It seemed to us that the sun itself rebelled against this injustice. What had our wives, children and mothers done to deserve this? Why all this? The beautiful, bright, radiant sun disappeared behind the clouds as if loath to look down upon our suffering and degradation.

Next came the command to board the train. As many as 80 persons were crowded into each car, with no way of escape. I was wearing only a pair of pants, a shirt and a pair of slippers. I had left at home a packed knapsack and a pair of boots which I had prepared because of rumors that we would be taken to the Ukraine and put to work there. Our train was shunted from one siding to another. Since I was familiar with this railroad junction I realized that our train was not moving out of the station. We were able to hear their shouts and **raucous**[5] laughter.

The air in the cars was becoming stiflingly hot and oppressive. It was difficult for us to breathe. Despair descended on us like a pall. I saw all of my companions in misery, but my mind was still unable to grasp the fate that lay in store for us. I had thought in terms of suffering, homelessness and hunger, but I still did not realize that the hangman's ruthless arm was threatening all of us, our children, our very existence.

At 4 P.M. the train started to move again and within a few minutes, we pulled into the Treblinka camp. Only when we arrived there did the full truth dawn on us in all its horror. Ukrainians armed with rifles and machine guns were stationed on the roofs of the barracks. The

---

[5] **raucous**—loud, disorderly.

camp yard was littered with corpses, some still in their clothes and others stark naked, their faces distorted with terror, black and swollen, the eyes wide open, with tongues protruding, skulls crushed, bodies mangled. And blood everywhere—the blood of innocent people, the blood of our children, of our brothers and sisters, our fathers and mothers.

Helpless, we intuitively felt that we would not be able to escape our destiny and would also become victims of our executioners. But what could be done about it? If only all this were just a nightmare! But no, it was stark reality. We were faced with what was termed "resettlement," but actually meant removal into the great beyond under untold tortures. We were ordered to get off the train and leave whatever packages we had in the cars.

* * *

They took us into the camp yard, which was flanked by barracks on either side. There were two large posters with big signs bearing instructions to surrender all gold, silver, diamonds, cash and other valuables under penalty of death. All the while Ukrainian guards stood on the roofs of the barracks, their machine guns at the ready.

The women and children were ordered to move to the left, and the men were told to line up at the right and squat on the ground. Some distance away from us a group of men was busy piling up our bundles, which they had taken from the trains. I managed to mingle with this group and began to work along with them. It was then that I received the first blow with a whip from a German whom we called Frankenstein. The women and children were ordered to undress, but I never found out what had become of the men. I never saw them again.

Late in the afternoon another train arrived from Miedzyrzec (Mezrich), but 80 per cent of its human cargo consisted of corpses. We had to carry them out of the train, under the whiplashes of the guards. At last we completed our gruesome chore. I asked one of my fellow workers what it meant. He merely replied that whoever you talk to today will not live to see tomorrow.

We waited in fear and suspense. After a while we were ordered to form a semi-circle. The Scharführer Franz walked up to us, accompanied by his dog and a Ukrainian guard armed with a machine gun. We were about 500 persons. We stood in mute suspense. About 100 of us were picked from the group, lined up five abreast, marched away some distance and ordered to kneel. I was one of those picked out. All of a sudden there was a roar of machine guns and the air was rent with the moans and screams of the victims. I never saw any of these people again. Under a rain of blows from whips and rifle butts the rest of us were driven into the barracks, which were dark and had no floors. I sat down on the sandy ground and dropped off to sleep.

When I arrived at the camp, three gas chambers were already in operation; another ten were added while I was there. A gas chamber measured 5 by 5 meters and was about 1.90 meters high. The outlet on the roof had a **hermetic**[6] cap. The chamber was equipped with a gas pipe inlet and a baked tile floor slanting towards the platform. The brick building which housed the gas chambers was separated from Camp No. 1 by a wooden wall. This wooden wall and the brick wall of the building together formed a corridor which was 80 centimeters taller than the building. The chambers were connected with the corridor by a hermetically fitted iron door leading into each of the chambers. On the side of Camp No. 2 the chambers were connected by a platform 4 meters wide, which ran alongside all three chambers. The

---

[6] **hermetic**—airtight.

platform was about 80 centimeters above ground level. There was also a hermetically fitted wooden door on this side.

Each chamber had a door facing Camp No. 2 (1.80 by 2.50 meters), which could be opened only from the outside by lifting it with iron supports and was closed by iron hooks set into the sash frames, and by wooden bolts. The victims were led into the chambers through the doors leading from the corridor, while the remains of the gassed victims were dragged out through the doors facing Camp No. 2. The power plant operated alongside these chambers, supplying Camps 1 and 2 with electric current. A motor taken from a dismantled Soviet tank stood in the power plant. This motor was used to pump the gas which was let into the chambers by connecting the motor with the inflow pipes. The speed with which death overcame the helpless victims depended on the quantity of combustion gas admitted into the chamber at one time.

The machinery of the gas chambers was operated by two Ukrainians. One of them, Ivan, was tall, and though his eyes seemed kind and gentle, he was a sadist. He enjoyed torturing his victims. He would often pounce upon us while we were working; he would nail our ears to the walls or make us lie down on the floor and whip us brutally. While he did this, his face showed sadistic satisfaction and he laughed and joked. He finished off the victims according to his mood at the moment. The other Ukrainian was called Nicholas. He had a pale face and the same mentality as Ivan.

The day I first saw men, women and children being led into the house of death I almost went insane. I tore at my hair and shed bitter tears of despair. I suffered most when I looked at the children, accompanied by their mothers or walking alone, entirely ignorant of the fact that within a few minutes their lives would be snuffed out amidst horrible tortures. Their eyes glittered with fear and still more, perhaps, with amazement. It seemed as if the question, "What is this? What's it all about?" was frozen on their lips. But seeing the stony expressions on the faces of their elders, they matched their behavior to the occasion. They either stood motionless or pressed tightly against each other or against their parents, and tensely awaited their horrible end.

Suddenly, the entrance door flew open and out came Ivan, holding a heavy gas pipe, and Nicholas, brandishing a saber. At a given signal, they would begin admitting the victims, beating them savagely as they moved into the chamber. The screams of the women, the weeping of the children, cries of despair and misery, the pleas for mercy, for God's vengeance ring in my ears to this day, making it impossible for me to forget the misery I saw.

Between 450 and 500 persons were crowded into a chamber measuring 25 square meters. Parents carried their children in their arms in the vain hope that this would save their children from death. On the way to their doom, they were pushed and beaten with rifle butts and with Ivan's gas pipe. Dogs were set upon them, barking, biting and tearing at them. To escape the blows and the dogs, the crowd rushed to its death, pushing into the chamber, the stronger ones shoving the weaker ones ahead of them. The bedlam lasted only a short while, for soon the doors were slammed shut. The chamber was filled, the motor turned on and connected with the inflow pipes and, within 25 minutes at the most, all lay stretched out dead or, to be more accurate, were standing up dead. Since there was not an inch of free space, they just leaned against each other.

They no longer shouted, because the thread of their lives had been cut off. They had no more needs or desires. Even in death, mothers held their children tightly in their arms. There were no more friends or foes. There was no more jealousy. All were equal. There was no longer any beauty or ugliness, for they all were yellow from the gas. There were no longer any rich or poor, for they all were equal before God's throne. And why all this? I keep asking myself that question. My life is hard, very hard. But I must live on to tell the world about all this barbarism.

As soon as the gassing was over, Ivan and Nicholas inspected the results, moved over to the other side, opened the door leading to the platform, and proceeded to heave out the corpses. It was our task to carry the corpses to the ditches. We were dead tired from working all day at the construction site, but we had no recourse and had no choice but to obey. We could have refused, but that would have meant a whipping or death in the same manner or even worse; so we obeyed without grumbling.

QUESTIONS TO CONSIDER

1. What factors prompted Wiernik to write his account? How does he feel about this task?

2. What is the dictionary meaning of the word *resettlement*? What did resettlement mean to the Jews?

3. How were so many Jews lured unsuspecting to their deaths?

The Verdict

BY SARA NOMBERG-PRZYTYK

A fifth death camp was built in the spring of 1942 at Auschwitz in Upper East Silesia. Auschwitz was already a functioning labor camp when the decision was made to build the gas chambers; the new camp at Auschwitz was known as Birkenau. Sara Nomberg-Przytyk was a Polish Jew born in 1915. After the German invasion, she lived in a ghetto and was sent to Auschwitz in 1943. She survived the camp and in the 1960s wrote a series of stories about her experiences. Auschwitz: True Tales from a Grotesque Land *tells the story of a young woman in a series of interconnected stories. "The Verdict" explores the issue of morality and survival in an inhuman situation.*

In October 1944 the whole hospital was moved to camp "C," the old gypsy camp. That is when I met Mrs. Helena. She had been doing the same job I was doing, except that she was a clerk in the infirmary for non-Jewish prisoners. In the new block, the separate infirmaries were liquidated and combined into one. The new infirmary was located in a separate barrack. In addition to the reception room there was a beautiful room containing three bunk beds. Five of the beds were occupied by the workers in the infirmary: Helena and I, the clerks; Mancy and Frieda, the two doctors; and nurse Marusia. The sixth bed was taken by Kwieta, who worked in the *Leichenkomando.*[1]

Mrs. Helena stuck out oddly in our group of five. Perhaps because she was older than we were, we felt very inhibited in her presence. She maintained a constant silence and seemed always to be steeped in her own thoughts. She lived her own life and said nothing to anyone. We did not even know how she had gotten to Auschwitz. She was slim, light-haired and had an **inscrutable**[2] face. She did not take part in our discussions, and she never judged anybody. She eavesdropped on our gossiping and seemed to be saying, "I would like to see how you would behave in a similar situation."

One evening, while we were discussing conscious and unconscious death, we were surprised to hear Helena break heatedly into our discussion:

"Listen to the story I am going to tell you about the death of 156 girls from Krakow, and then you can tell me what you think of the way I behaved." We all stopped talking, and complete silence descended on our cell.

"We were just finishing receiving the sick," Mrs. Helena started quietly. "While Mengele[3] was looking over the women who had been admitted to the area, we had but one thought in our minds: we hoped he would leave soon. I remember that it was a scorching July day. The atmosphere in the infirmary was almost unbearable. The last sick woman moved through the line, passing in front of the German doctor. We heaved a sigh of relief. Mengele got up slowly, buttoned his

---

[1] *Leichenkomando*—corpse squad, those responsible for transporting the bodies of the dead.

[2] **inscrutable**—cannot be understood; so mysterious or obscure that one cannot make out its meaning.

[3] Mengele—also known as the "Angel of Death," Josef Mengele did medical experiments on the inmates at Auschwitz.

uniform, stood facing me, and said: 'At fifteen hours the *Leichenauto*[4] will come; I will come at fourteen hours.' We looked at one another in dumb amazement. Why the Leichenauto at fifteen hours? Usually, the car came to pick up the dead after darkness had fallen. What was Mengele planning to do here at fourteen hours? We couldn't speak. We were all sure that the *Leichenauto* was coming for us, to take us to the crematorium. We had to start cleaning up, but you can believe that everything kept dropping out of our hands, and that the hours dragged on without end. It's not easy to wait for the worst. After all, I don't have to tell you about that.

"At thirteen hours two young girls came to the infirmary, Poles from Krakow. They told us that the *blokowa*[5] had ordered them to report here because they had to leave for work in Germany and Mengele was going to examine them. I was so frightened by what I heard that I almost fainted. 'Is it only you the *blokowa* sent?' I asked in a quivering voice.

"'Not just us,' they answered. 'There will be a lot more of us here. The rest will be coming soon. We came in first because we are in a hurry to join the transport that is leaving Auschwitz.'

"Quite a large number of women were now gathering in front of the infirmary, most of them young. They were happy to be leaving Auschwitz. They were talking loudly, laughing, never dreaming that they had been horribly deceived and that the *Leichenauto* was coming for them in about an hour. For us it was all clear; those Poles were condemned to death, and the sentence was going to be carried out in the infirmary. 'What to do?' I thought feverishly. Maybe I should tell them why they had been summoned here. Perhaps I should shout it out to them: 'Calm down! Don't laugh. You are living corpses,

---

[4] *Leichenauto*—vehicle used to transport corpses.

[5] *blokowa*—prisoner head of a women's barrack.

and in a few hours nothing will be left of you but ashes!' Then what? Then we attendants would go to the gas chambers and the women would die anyway. The women might run and scatter all over the camp, but in the end they would get caught. Their numbers have been recorded. There is no place for them to run.

"Believe me, we quietly took counsel, trying to decide what to do. We didn't tell them the terrible truth, not out of fear for our own lives, but because we truly did not know what would be the least painful way for the young women to die. Now they didn't know anything, they were carefree, and death would be upon them before they knew it. If we told them what was in store for them, then a struggle for life would ensue. In their attempt to run from death they would find only loneliness, because their friends, seeking to preserve their own lives, would refuse to help them. There were more than 150 women in front of the infirmary. They stood in rows of five, as at roll call, and waited for the doctor to examine them. Still, we did not know what to do. All our reasoning told us to say nothing. Today I know that it was fear for our own lives that made us reason this way, that induced us to believe that sudden, unexpected death is preferable to a death that makes itself known to your full and open consciousness.

"Precisely at fourteen hours, Mengele arrived, accompanied by an orderly named Kler. He looked at the lines of women standing there and then at us in such a way as to make us partners in the crimes that he was about to commit. At that moment I knew that we had made a mistake in not telling the young women what was awaiting them. Whether dying is supposed to be easy or difficult, I suppose every individual has to decide for herself. But it was our duty to inform the young women what awaited them.

"'Bring them in for a checkup,' shouted Mengele. The first girl walked in, the one who was in a hurry to leave Auschwitz. She stood in front of me; I did not say anything. By filling out her hospital card, I was taking part in this deception that was making it easy for Mengele to execute his victim. She walked in without suspecting anything. Then I heard the crashing sound of a falling body; later, the second; then the third, the tenth, the twentieth. Always the same: the card, the squeaking of the door, the crash of a falling body. The corpses were thrown out into the waiting room, which was located behind the reception room. An SS man with a dog kept order in front of the infirmary. Calm and trusting, the women kept going in. I lowered my head so they wouldn't see my face. All I would see each time was a hand stretched out to receive a card. I really did not understand why they were so calm. Weren't they surprised not to see the other women coming out of the infirmary after they had been examined? I looked for some sign of anxiety in those stretched out hands, but to no avail. I had given out about a hundred cards when it started.

"One of the girls asked the SS man why the other women weren't coming out after having been examined. Instead of answering her he hit her over the head with his rifle butt. Then I heard one of the girls yell, 'We are not going in there. They will give us an injection of phenol.'[6] A terrible outcry started. The girls really refused to enter the infirmary. When one of them tried to run away the SS man shot her. At the sound of a shot a whole troop of SS men and dogs ran in. The young women were completely surrounded. Each girl, having first been beaten, was dragged screaming, by two SS men, into the presence of Mengele. I didn't give out any more cards. It was no longer necessary.

---

[6] phenol—carbolic acid.

"I jumped up from my seat and hid in a corner of the infirmary. The women did not want to die. They tore themselves out of the grip of the SS men and started to run away. Then the dogs were set on them. Their deaths were completely different from the deaths of the first batch of women who went to their deaths unknowing. Who knows which death was more difficult, but the first group seemed to die more peacefully.

"At fifteen hours the *Leichenauto* showed up, and an hour later the entire operation was completed. Up to the very last minute we were not certain that Mengele was not going to send us, the witnesses of that bloody happening, to the gas. Mengele left, calm, and with a smile he put down the sick card he had been holding. 'Herzanfall [heart attack],' he said."

Mrs. Helena finished her terrible tale. We did not utter a word. After a long pause she resumed: "I still don't know whether we should have told the women about the death that was waiting for them. What do you think?"

None of us said anything.

QUESTIONS TO CONSIDER

1. Why did Mrs. Helena originally decide not to tell the girls what was going to happen to them?

2. How does Mrs. Helena feel about her role in the deaths of the girls? What was she afraid would happen as a result of her witnessing these deaths?

3. At the end of her story, Mrs. Helena says, "I still don't know whether we should have told the women about the death that was waiting for them. What do you think?" How would you answer this question?

from

A Man for Others

BY PATRICIA TREECE

Raymond Kolbe (1894–1941) was born near Lodz in Poland. In 1910, he joined the Franciscan order of the Catholic Church, taking the name Maximilian. Kolbe was famed for his kindliness, self-command, and his dedication to the Franciscan beliefs in poverty, preaching, and missionary work. When the Germans occupied Poland in 1939, Kolbe began to write about the atrocities he saw being perpetrated. He was harassed and arrested, and, finally in 1941, sent to Auschwitz. Kolbe suffered from tuberculosis, but as a Christian, he was used as a slave laborer rather than sent to the gas chambers. In Auschwitz, attempts at escape were discouraged by the execution of a group of people from the cell block of any escapee. Kolbe volunteered to take the place of a man chosen for death in such a reprisal. He and the others chosen were sealed in a cell, naked, and left to starve to death. Still not dead after two weeks, Kolbe was killed by lethal injection. In 1982, the Catholic Church made Kolbe an official saint.

As July came to an end, the next feast of the Mother of God, that of her assumption into heaven, lay fifteen days away. With harvest season in full swing, one prisoner assigned to swell the farm details began dreaming of escape through the open fields. Joseph Sobolewski, who arrived at Auschwitz in August 1940 as number 2,877 in the first Warsaw transport, recalls that there had already been two prisoners that summer who successfully fled that way. But the Nazis made sure such events were no occasion for rejoicing among those left behind. It took a certain kind of desperation to run away, knowing what others would pay. On almost the last day of July, the dreamer had become that desperate. Francis Mleczko remembers:

> We were working digging gravel (to be used in building more Blocks) outside the camp when suddenly, about three in the afternoon, the sirens began to wail and shriek. That was a terrible sign. It meant there had been an escape. At once the German sentries lifted their guns, counted us, and began to keep an extra strict watch. Besides scrutinizing our every movement, the guards were also alert for any sign of the escapee who might be hiding, for all they knew, in a field, a tree, on a floor, inside a vehicle, or any one of a thousand places.
>
> The siren's crescendo not only alerted the SS[1] and capos[2] outside the camp, it even reached the villages outside the fifteen-mile penal zone, warning the police to set up roadblocks and watch for the poor fugitive. The thoughts of all of us were not on him, however, but ourselves; for if the escapee was from our Block, we knew

---

[1] SS— Nazis who served as Hitler's bodyguard and as a policing unit of the German army.

[2] capos—commanders.

ten to twenty of us would die in **reprisal.**[3] So I prayed, and I imagine everyone else was doing the same: "Oh please don't let him be from my Block. Let him be from Block 3 or Block 8 but not from 14. . . ."

To the assembled, fear-stricken eyes looking directly at him because they have no choice, Fritsch barks, "The fugitive has not been found. In reprisal for your comrade's escape, ten of you will die by starvation. Next time, it will be twenty." Immediately the selection begins. Palitsch and a prisoner-secretary precede him with pad and pencil to take down the numbers of the condemned; Fritsch walks down the first row of identically garbed, nameless men. He meanders slowly to prolong their terror. Perhaps he is even so sick that he enjoys the feeling that each life is momentarily his to dangle helplessly before its owner before setting it down or shattering it forever. He scrutinizes faces. Then, with a gesture, he chooses his first victim from the front row. This does not mean the rest in that line are safe, however. He might take another. Even when the tenth man is chosen, the SS had been known to go on and take eleven, twelve, thirteen—as many as eighteen. After the first row is inspected, the order is given: "Three paces forward." They move up, leaving an alley between them and the second row so the arrogant Fritsch can one by one, stare each of these hapless souls straight in the face, while musing with leisurely care on his fate. . . .

Finally the grisly selection is complete. Fritsch turns to Palitsch, the noncommissioned officer who likes to brag about the numbers he has shot at the execution wall by Block 11. Together the SS officers check the secretary's list against the numbers on the condemned. As their German passion for accuracy occupies them, one

---

[3] **reprisal**—injury done in return for injury.

of the victims is sobbing, "My wife and my children!" It is Francis Gajowniczek. The SS ignore him.

Suddenly, there is movement in the still ranks. A prisoner several rows back has broken out and is pushing his way toward the front. The SS guards watching this Block raise their automatic rifles, while the dogs at their heels tense for the order to spring. Fritsch and Palitsch too reach toward their holsters. The prisoner steps past the first row.

It is Kolbe. His step is firm, his face peaceful. Angrily, the Block capo shouts at him to stop or be shot. Kolbe answers calmly, "I want to talk to the commander," and keeps on walking while the capo, oddly enough, neither shoots nor clubs him. Then, still at a respectful distance, Kolbe stops, his cap in his hands. Standing at attention like an officer of some sort himself, he looks Fritsch straight in the eye.

"Herr Kommandant, I wish to make a request, please," he says politely in flawless German.

Survivors will later say it is a miracle that no one shoots him. Instead, Fritsch asks, "What do you want?"

"I want to die in place of this prisoner," and Kolbe points toward the sobbing Gajowniczek. He presents this **audacious**[4] request without a stammer. Fritsch looks stupefied, irritated. Everyone notes how the German lord of life and death, suddenly nervous, actually steps back a pace.

The prisoner explains coolly, as if they were discussing some everyday matter, that the man over there has a family.

"I have no wife or children. Besides, I'm old and not good for anything. He's in better condition," he adds, adroitly playing on the Nazi line that only the fit should live.

"Who are you?" Fritsch croaks.

"A Catholic priest."

---

[4] **audacious**—bold.

Fritsch is silent. The stunned Block, audience to this drama, expect him in usual Auschwitz fashion to show no mercy but sneer, "Well, since you're so eager, we'll just let you come along too," and take both men. Instead, after a moment, the deputy-commander snaps, "Request granted." As if he needs to expel some fury, he kicks Gajowniczek, snarling, "Back to ranks, you!"

Prisoners in ranks are never allowed to speak. Gajowniczek says:

> I could only try to thank him with my eyes. I was stunned and could hardly grasp what was going on. The immensity of it: I, the condemned, am to live and someone else willingly and voluntarily offers his life for me—a stranger. Is this some dream or reality? . . .

Now the order is given for the condemned to march and then the Block is dismissed. Brother Ladislaus says:

> The ten victims walked in front of me and I saw that Father Kolbe was staggering under the weight of one of the others as he upheld this man who could not walk with his own strength.

Some of his buddies rush over to Ted Wotjkowski, who is still dazed, benumbed by his own near death-sentence and by the sacrifice he has just seen. "C'mon, let's forget it," they urge, but Ted stands there as if paralyzed still. He is thinking, "I've just seen a saint made."

* * *

The heart of every Catholic institution is the chapel with its tabernacle housing the living God. From there, believers feel powerful, sweet radiations.

Auschwitz, too, had a spiritual heart from which radiated agony, despair, and death. This was the prison within the prison, the penal Block called the bunker, where in the basement the SS "interrogated" prisoners with unspeakable cruelty. In one of these cells, made airtight for the occasion, the first gassings would be done on hapless hospital patients, Jews and Russian prisoners of war.

It was here Kolbe entered like a sliver of light into a black pit. He who without prudery was so modest was naked. The SS guard had snarled, "Strip," while they were still outside the Block. No sense in his having to carry their garments up the stairs. Then it was in the door of the innocent-looking brick building and descent into the dark, **fetid**[5] basement where they were shoved into one of the rank-smelling cells.

"You'll dry up like tulips," their jailer sneered as he slammed the door.

How do we know? Former SS men do not exactly come forward in droves to testify to their heartlessness. Their victims are dead.

There were, however, prisoner secretary-interpreters even in this infamous Block 11. To ensure their silence on what went on there, these men were liquidated from time to time like the later crematorium workers.

By some act of God, the prisoner-interpreter who would watch Kolbe's last days came out of Auschwitz alive. Number 1,192, Bruno Borgowiec was a Pole from Silesia, the rich, coal-mining region whose ownership has changed hands among several countries, including Germany and Poland. He worked with the other earliest prisoners building the camp; then, because of his perfect German, he was given the very dangerous job of interpreter in the penal Block. One can only imagine the things he was forced to see, to hear. Suffice it to say Bruno Borgowiec died on the Monday after Easter in 1947, when he was only about forty years old. But not

---

[5] **fetid**—having a heavy offensive smell.

before he had written Niepokalanow on December 27, 1945, with many details of what he had seen and left two notarized, sworn statements, one brief, the other more detailed, of the last days of the man he considered "a hero and a saint."

It is Borgowiec who provides the details of what those who know Kolbe would suspect: The starvation cell, far from defeating him, would become a tabernacle in this cruelest part of Auschwitz, as if—hidden in the heart of the humble Franciscan—God had snuck into Hell.

Borgowiec explains why he could repeat even the SS man's cruel jest as he locked the victims into their death cell, where only a tiny window high up against the basement ceiling let in a little light. In spite of thousands having died in that bunker, he remembered even such isolated details about Father Kolbe's last days "with absolute clarity," he maintained, "because of the absolutely extraordinary behavior with which the noble Father faced death." I combine Borgowiec's various reports:

> The naked victims were in one cell near those [dying in reprisal because] of the two previous escapes. The foul air was horrible, the cell floor cement. There was no furniture whatsoever, except for a bucket for relieving themselves.
>
> You could say Father Kolbe's presence in the bunker was necessary for the others. They were in a frenzy over the thoughts of never returning to their homes and families, screaming in despair and cursing. He pacified them and they [began to] resign themselves. With his gift of consolation, he prolonged the lives of the condemned who were usually so psychologically destroyed that they succumbed in just a few days.

To keep up their spirits, he encouraged them that the escapee might still be found and they would be released. [Koscielniak talked to the German Streiberg and the bunker chief, who told him Kolbe was hearing the victims' confessions and preparing them to die.] So they could join him, he prayed aloud. The cell doors were made of oak. Because of the silence and acoustics, the voice of Father Kolbe in prayer was diffused to the other cells, where it could be heard well. These prisoners joined in.

From then on, every day from the cell where these poor souls were joined by the adjoining cells, one heard the recitation of prayers, the rosary, and hymns. Father Kolbe led while the others responded as a group. As these fervent prayers and hymns resounded in all corners of the bunker, I had the impression I was in a church.

Outside the penal Block, Francis Mleczko recalls that the prisoners were keeping a kind of prayer vigil in their free hours, walking past the tiny window where only the top of a head could be seen. Szweda had even rashly gone to the death Block to inquire. He was growled at by a prisoner who worked there, "You fool, don't you know better than to ask questions like that? Do you want to end up here too? Run away fast before someone sees you."

Borgowiec continues:

Once a day the SS men in charge of the penal Block inspected the cells, ordering me to carry away the corpses of those who had died during the night. I also always had to be present for these inspections because, as secretary-interpreter, it was my job to write down the numbers of the dead and also to translate from Polish into German any conversation or questions asked by the condemned.

Sometimes Father Kolbe's group was so deeply absorbed in prayer that they didn't notice the SS opening the door. It took loud shouts to get their attention. When they saw the cell door was opened, the poor wretches, weeping, would loudly beg for a crust of bread and some water, which they never obtained. If one of those who still had the strength approached the door, right away the SS would kick the poor man in the stomach so [hard] that falling back on the cement floor he would die or, if not, they would shoot him.

Father Kolbe never asked for anything and he never complained.

He looked directly and intently into the eyes of those entering the cell. Those eyes of his were always strangely penetrating. The SS men couldn't stand his glance, and used to yell at him, "Schau auf die Erde, nicht auf uns!" ("Look at the ground, not at us.")

Physician Francis Wlodarski was also told by a Nazi patient, the penal bunker chief, with whom he maintained good relations in order to get news, that Kolbe was "a psychic trauma, a shock" for the SS men who had to bear his look—a look that hungered (not that the penal chief put it this way) not for bread but to liberate them from evil. This Nazi's evaluation of Kolbe: "An extremely courageous man, really a superhuman hero." Borgowiec continues:

I overheard the SS talking about him among themselves. They were admiring his courage and behavior. One of them said, "So einen wie diesen Pfarrer haben wir hier noch nicht gehabt. Das muss ein ganz aussergewöhnlicher Mensch sein." ("We've never had a priest here like this one. He must be a wholly exceptional man.")

While the SS men were absent, I used to go down and console my countrymen. [Through the keyhole or the hinged observation window, Borgowiec also passed Kolbe's group vitamin C, which he got from friends in the hospital; after awhile he desisted, realizing that if he were extending their lives, he was only prolonging their agony.]

What kind of martyrdom these men were enduring can be imagined from the fact that the urine bucket was always dry. In their dreadful thirst, they must have drunk its contents.

As the prisoners became weaker, the prayers continued, but in whispers. But even when during each inspection the others were always found lying on the cement, Father Kolbe was still standing or kneeling, his face serene.

In this way, two weeks went by. The prisoners were dying one after the other, and by this time only four were left, among them Father Kolbe, who was still conscious. The SS decided things were taking too long. . . . One day they sent for the German criminal Bock from the hospital to give the prisoners injections of carbolic acid. After the needle prick in the vein of the left arm, you could follow the instant swelling as it moved up the arm toward the chest. When it reached the heart, the victim would fall dead. Between injection and death was a little more than ten seconds.

When Bock got there, I had to accompany them to the cell. I saw Father Kolbe, with a prayer, himself hold out his arm to the executioner. I couldn't bear it. With the excuse that I had some work to do, I left. But as soon as the SS and their executioner were gone, I returned.

The other naked, begrimed corpses were lying on the floor, their faces betraying signs of their sufferings. Father Kolbe was sitting upright, leaning against the far wall. His body was not dirty like the others, but clean and bright. The head was tilted somewhat to one side. His eyes were open. Serene and pure, his face was radiant.

Anybody would have noticed and thought this was some saint.

QUESTIONS TO CONSIDER

1. What offer does Kolbe make? What surprises the other prisoners about Kolbe's offer and the commander's reaction to it?

2. How does Father Kolbe help the men who are sentenced to die of starvation?

3. What effect does Kolbe have on the entire camp?

The Concentration Camps

▲
The entrance to the concentration camp at Dachau, seen here after liberation by the American army.

◄ The electrified fence surrounding the barracks for the prisoners at the Lublin camp.

▲
Polish women being led to their execution.

◀ Poles who have been chosen for death, being rounded up at a
concentration camp.

The ovens at Dachau that were used to consume the corpses of prisoners.
This oven on the left shows evidence of a human corpse.
▼

The Perpetrators
of the Holocaust

Chelmno

Chelmno is the remote Polish village where the Germans began regular gassings of Jews and Gypsies. On December 7, 1941, 700 Jews were murdered in mobile gas vans. From that date, gassings were a daily occurrence; more than 360,000 Jews and Gypsies were killed by the end of 1942 at Chelmno. This was not a concentration camp, but a place solely designed to annihilate those who were brought to it. The book "The Good Old Days": The Holocaust as Seen by the Perpetrators and Bystanders *is a collection of testimonies, albums, and documents from the people who ran the death camps at Chelmno and Treblinka. The following is a series of excerpts from testimony by German soldiers who served at Chelmno.*

Between December 1941 and March 1943 at least 145,000 people—according to criminal proceedings in the Laabs et al. (8 Ks 3/62) trial in Bonn on 23 July 1965—were murdered here in gas-vans. On 7 April 1943 the "castle" was blown up. Between April 1944 and January 1945 several thousand more people were killed. Polish estimates put the total number of victims as high as 300,000.

Theodor Malzmüller on the "Plague Boils of Humanity"

When we arrived we had to report to the camp commandant, SS-Hauptsturmführer Bothmann. The SS-Hauptsturmführer addressed us in his living quarters, in the presence of SS-Untersturmführer Albert Plate (Bothmann's deputy). He explained that we had been detailed to the Kulmhof [Chelmno] extermination camp as guards and added that in this camp the plague boils of humanity, the Jews, were exterminated. We were to keep quiet about everything we saw or heard, otherwise we would have to reckon with our families' imprisonment and the death penalty.

We were then allocated our places in the guard unit [Wachkommando], which consisted of about fifty to sixty police officers from 1st Company Litzmannstadt Police Battalion. As I recall, there were also some officers from 2nd Company in it. The officer in charge of the guard unit was Oberleutnant Gustav Hüfing. He was from Wesel. . . .

The guardroom was situated in the village of Kulmhof. The unit members were accommodated in houses in the village The duties of the guard unit consisted of (1) maintaining the security of the guardroom, (2) guarding the so-called "castle" yard and (3) guarding the so-called "camp in the wood."

The extermination camp was made up of the so-called "castle" and the camp in the wood. The castle was a fairly large stone building at the edge of the village of Kulmhof. It was here that the Jews who had been transported by lorry or railway were first brought. The Jews were addressed by a member of the Sonderkommando in the castle courtyard. I myself once heard one of these speeches when I was on guard duty in the castle courtyard for a day in December 1942. . . .

When a lorry had arrived the following members of the SS-Sonderkommando addressed the Jews: (1) camp commandant Bothmann, (2) SS-Untersturmführer Albert

Plate from North Germany, (3) Polizei-Meister Willi Lenz from Silesia, (4) Polizei-Meister Alois Häberle from Württemberg. They explained to the Jews that they would first of all be given a bath and deloused in Kulmhof and then sent to Germany "to work." The Jews then went inside the castle. There they had to get undressed. After this they were sent through a passage-way on to a ramp to the castle yard where the so-called "gas-van" was parked. The back door of the van would be open. The Jews were made to get inside the van. This job was done by three Poles, who I believe were sen-tenced to death. The Poles hit the Jews with whips if they did not get into the gas van fast enough. When all the Jews were inside, the door was bolted. The driver then switched on the engine, crawled under the van and connected a pipe from the exhaust to the inside of the van. The exhaust fumes now poured into the inside of the truck so that the people inside were suffocated. After about ten minutes, when there were no further signs of life from the Jews, the van set off towards the camp in the wood where the bodies were then burnt. . . .

During the period that I was in the guard unit most of the time I did sentry duty in the interior of the camp in the wood. The camp was in a clearing in the woods between Kulmhof and Warthbrücken. . . . As a guard just within the camp perimeter I frequently saw mass graves, filled with the bodies of Jews who had been exterminated, being dug up by the Jewish Arbeitskommando. The bodies were then burnt in two incinerators. . . .

At the end of March 1943, shortly before the dismantling of Kulmhof extermination camp in April, Gauleiter Greiser suddenly appeared at the camp togeth-er with his staff (consisting of fifteen high-ranking SS officers). All members of the SS-Sonderkommando and the Wachkommando had to assemble in the courtyard of the castle where they were addressed by Greiser. In the presence of his staff he explained that Kulmhof extermination camp would shortly be dismantled and he wanted to thank us on behalf of the Führer for the work we had done in Kulmhof. He went on to say that everybody would be given four weeks' special leave and that we were welcome to spend it free of charge on one of his estates. He then invited all those present to a farewell party at a hotel in Warthbrücken. The farewell party was held in a big room in the hotel. After a short while everyone was drunk and fell asleep at the table. The party ended at about one or two in the morning. . . .

A few days after Greiser's farewell party all members of the SS-Sonderkommando and the police guards received four weeks' special leave. Only a few members of the SS-Sonderkommando stayed behind in Kulmhof. One of these was Polizei-Meister Lenz. Then everybody had to report to SS-Obergruppenführer Kaltenbrunner at state security headquarters in Berlin on a particular day. He addressed us all and we were once again thanked on behalf of the Führer for our work in Kulmhof.

We were then all detailed together to Yugoslavia to SS-Division Prinz Eugen, under the command of Bothmann. Here we were deployed against **partisans**[1] in Yugoslavia and suffered very heavy losses. As far as I can recall, SS-Untersturmführer Plate committed suicide in Serbia after being severely wounded.

In the middle of 1944 some of those former members of the SS-Sonderkommando who were still alive were withdrawn from the SS Division and sent back to Kulmhof to start up the extermination camp once again.

Gas-van Driver Walter Burmeister on Whether He Ever Thought About What He Was Doing

As soon as the ramp had been erected in the castle, people started arriving in Kulmhof from Litzmannstadt in lorries[2]. . . . The people were told that they had to take

---

[1] **partisans**—strong supporters of a person or cause.
[2] lorries—British term for trucks.

a bath, that their clothes had to be disinfected and that they could hand in any valuable items beforehand to be registered. On the instructions of Kommandoführer Lange [Bothmann's predecessor] I also had to give a similar talk in the castle to the people waiting there— how often exactly I can no longer say today. The purpose of the talk was to keep the people in the dark about what lay before them. When they had undressed they were sent to the cellar of the castle and then along a passageway on to the ramp and from there into the gas-van. In the castle there were signs marked "To the baths." The gas-vans were large vans about 4-5 m long, 2.20 m wide and 2 m high. The interior walls were lined with sheet metal. On the floor there was a wooden grille. The floor of the van had an opening which could be connected to the exhaust by means of a removable metal pipe. When the lorries were full of people the double doors at the back were closed and the exhaust connected to the interior of the van. . . .

The Kommando member detailed as driver would start the engine straight away so that the people inside the lorry were suffocated by the exhaust gases. Once this had taken place, the union between the exhaust and the inside of the lorry was disconnected and the van was driven to the camp in the woods where the bodies were unloaded. In the early days they were initially buried in mass graves, later incinerated. . . . I then drove the van back to the castle and parked it there. Here it would be cleaned of the excretions of the people that had died in it. Afterwards it would once again be used for gassings. . . .

I can no longer say today what I thought at the time or whether I thought of anything at all. I can also no longer say today whether I was too influenced by the **propaganda**[3] of the time to have refused to have carried out the orders I had been given.

---

[3] **propaganda**—systematic effort to spread opinions or beliefs.

Kurt Möbius on the Guilt of the Jews and His Own Lack of Blame

. . . In addition Hauptsturmführer Lange said to us that the orders to exterminate the Jews had been issued by Hitler and Himmler.[4] We had been drilled in such a way that we viewed all orders issued by the head of state as lawful and correct. We police went by the phrase, "Whatever serves the state is right, whatever harms the state is wrong." I would also like to say that it never even entered my head that these orders could be wrong. Although I am aware that it is the duty of the police to protect the innocent I was however at that time convinced that the Jewish people were not innocent but guilty. I believed all the propaganda that Jews were criminals and subhuman [Untermenschen] and that they were the cause of Germany's decline after the First World War. The thought that one should oppose or evade the order to take part in the extermination of the Jews never entered my head either. I followed these orders because they came from the highest leaders of the state and not because I was in any way afraid.

Interrogation of Adolf Eichmann[5]

E   I just know the following, that I only saw the following: a room, if I still recall correctly, perhaps five times as big as this one, or it may have been four times as big. There were Jews inside it, they had to get undressed and then a van, completely sealed, drew up to a ramp in front of the entrance. The naked Jews then had to get inside. Then the lorry was closed and it drove off.

L   How many people did the van hold?

---

[4] Himmler, Heinrich—director of Nazi propaganda from 1926-1930, who eventually became head of all German police forces.

[5] Eichmann, Adolf—SS officer who directed the roundups of Jews and their transport to concentration and death camps.

E I can't say exactly. I couldn't bring myself to look
closely, even once. I didn't look inside the entire
time. I couldn't, no, I couldn't take any more.
The screaming and, and, I was too upset and so
on. I also said that to [SS-Obergruppenführer]
Müller when I submitted my report.

He did not get very much from my report. I
then followed the van—I must have been with
some of the people from there who knew the
way. Then I saw the most horrifying thing I have
ever seen in my entire life.

The van drove up to a long trench, the doors
were opened and bodies thrown out. They still
seemed alive, their limbs were so supple. They
were thrown in, I can still remember a civilian
pulling out teeth with some pliers and then I just
got the hell out of there. I got into the car, went
off and did not say anything else. . . . I'd had
more than I could take. I only know that a
doctor there in a white coat said to me that I
should look through a peep-hole at them in the
lorry. I refused to do that. I could not, I could not
say anything, I had to get away.

I went to Berlin, reported to Gruppenführer
Müller. I told him exactly what I've just said,
there wasn't any more I could tell him. . . .
Terrible . . . I'm telling you . . . the inferno, can't,
that is, I can't take this, I said to him.

Gauleiter Greiser to Himmler, 19 March 1943
Reichsführer!

A few days ago I visited Lange's former Sonderkommando, which today is under the command of SS-Haup
-tsturmführer Kriminalkommissar Bothmann and
stationed in Kulmhof, Kreis Warthbrücken, until the
end of the month. During my visit I was so struck by the
conduct of the men of the Sonderkommando that I

would not like to fail to bring it to your attention. The men have not only fulfilled the difficult task that has been set for them loyally, bravely and in all respects appropriately, but also their soldierly conduct is exemplary.

For example during a social evening to which I had invited them they gave me a contribution of 15,150 RM in cash which they had that day collected spontaneously. That means that each of these eighty-five men in the Sonderkommando had contributed about 180 RM. I have given instructions for the money to be put in the fund set up for the children of murdered ethnic Germans, unless you, Reichsführer, wish it to be put to another or better use.

The men further expressed the wish that all of them, if possible, be put under the command of their Hauptsturmführer Bothmann when they are transferred to their new assignment. I promised the men that I would communicate this wish to you, Reichsführer.

I should be grateful it you would give me permission to invite some of these men to be my guests on my country estate during their leave and to give them a generous allowance to make their leave more enjoyable.

Heil Hitler

(signed) Greiser

QUESTIONS TO CONSIDER

1. What role did propaganda play in the annihilation of the Jews?

2. What is Adolf Eichmann's attitude toward his participation in the killing of the Jews? How does he describe his role in the killing?

3. In Greiser's letter, he mentions that soldiers gave him money that they had "collected." From where do you think this money came? What use does Greiser suggest for the money? Why does he feel this is justifiable?

Commanding a Concentration Camp

BY RUDOLF HÖSS

Rudolf Höss (1900–1947) was a German who found his calling in the army during World War I. Dismayed by post-war Germany, he joined the Nazi Party in 1922 and became a member of the SS in 1934. Höss was sent to serve at Dachau, the earliest of the Nazi concentration camps, which had been founded in 1933. Höss was an exemplary officer at Dachau and later Sachsenhausen. In 1941, he was chosen to oversee the creation of Auschwitz and, in his own words, turned it into "the greatest human extermination center of all time." Höss was condemned and executed by a Polish court in 1947. Before his execution, he wrote an account of his experiences which was published as Commandant of Auschwitz *in 1951. Below is an excerpt from his chilling account of how genocide is perpetrated.*

By the will of the Reichsführer SS, Auschwitz became the greatest human extermination center of all time.

When in the summer of 1941 he himself gave me the order to prepare installations at Auschwitz where mass exterminations could take place, and personally to carry out these exterminations, I did not have the slightest idea of their scale or consequences. It was certainly an extraordinary and monstrous order. Nevertheless the reasons behind the extermination program seemed to me right. I did not reflect on it at the time: I had been given an order, and I had to carry it out. Whether this mass extermination of the Jews was necessary or not was something on which I could not allow myself to form an opinion, for I lacked the necessary breadth of view.

If the Führer had himself given the order for the "final solution of the Jewish question," then, for a veteran National-Socialist and even more so for an SS officer, there could be no question of considering its merits. "The Führer commands, we follow," was never a mere phrase or slogan. It was meant in bitter earnest.

Since my arrest it has been said to me repeatedly that I could have disobeyed this order, and that I might even have assassinated Himmler.[1] I do not believe that of all the thousands of SS[2] officers there could have been found a single one capable of such a thought. It was completely impossible. Certainly many SS officers grumbled and complained about some of the harsh orders that came from the Reichsführer SS, but they nevertheless always carried them out.

Many orders of the Reichsführer SS deeply offended a great number of his SS officers, but I am perfectly certain that not a single one of them would have dared to raise a hand against him, or would have even contemplated doing so in his most secret thoughts. As Reichsführer SS, his person was **inviolable**.[3] His basic

---

[1] Himmler—Heinrich Himmler, director of Nazi propaganda from 1926-1930, who eventually became head of all German police forces.

[2] SS— Nazis who served as Hitler's bodyguard and as a policing unit of the German army.

[3] **inviolable**—someone or something that cannot be violated or injured.

orders, issued in the name of the Führer, were sacred. They brooked no consideration, no argument, no interpretation. They were carried out ruthlessly and regardless of consequences, even though these might well mean the death of the officer concerned, as happened to not a few SS officers during the war.

It was not for nothing that during training the self-sacrifice of the Japanese for their country and their emperor, who was also their god, was held up as a shining example to the SS.

SS training was not comparable to a university course which can have as little lasting effect on the students as water on a duck's back. It was on the contrary something that was deeply engrained, and the Reichsführer SS knew very well what he could demand of his men.

But outsiders simply cannot understand that there was not a single SS officer who would disobey an order from the Reichsführer SS, far less consider getting rid of him because of the gruesomely hard nature of one such order.

What the Führer, or in our case his second-in-command, the Reichsführer SS, ordered was always right.

Democratic England also has a basic national concept: "My Country, right or wrong!" and this is adhered to by every nationally-conscious Englishman.

Before the mass extermination of the Jews began, the Russian *politruks* and political commissars were liquidated in almost all the concentration camps during 1941 and 1942.

In accordance with a secret order issued by Hitler, these Russian politruks and political commissars were combed out of all the prisoner-of-war camps by special detachments from the Gestapo. When identified, they were transferred to the nearest concentration camp for liquidation. It was made known that these measures were taken because the Russians had been killing all German soldiers who were party members or belonged to special sections of the NSDAP,[4] especially members of the SS, and also because the political officials of the Red Army[5] had been ordered, if taken prisoner, to create every kind of disturbance in the prisoner-of-war camps and their places of employment and to carry out sabotage wherever possible.

The political officials of the Red Army thus identified were brought to Auschwitz for liquidation. The first, smaller transports of them were executed by firing squads.

While I was away on duty, my deputy, Fritzsch, the commander of the protective custody camp, first tried gas for these killings. It was a preparation of prussic acid, called Cyclon B, which was used in the camp as an insecticide and of which there was always a stock on hand. On my return, Fritzsch reported this to me, and the gas was used again for the next transport.

The gassing was carried out in the detention cells of Block II. Protected by a gas-mask, I watched the killing myself. In the crowded cells death came instantaneously the moment the Cyclon B was thrown in. A short, almost smothered cry, and it was all over. During this first experience of gassing people, I did not fully realize what was happening, perhaps because I was too impressed by the whole procedure. I have a clearer recollection of the gassing of nine hundred Russians which took place shortly afterwards in the old crematorium, since the use of Block II for this purpose caused too much trouble. While the transport was detraining, holes were pierced in the earth and concrete ceiling of the mortuary. The Russians were ordered to undress in an anteroom; they then quietly entered the mortuary, for

---

[4] NSDAP—abbreviation for National Socialist German Workers' Party, also called the Nazi Party, which was initiated in 1920. Adolf Hitler had control of the Nazi Party from 1933-1945.

[5] Red Army—also known as the Soviet Army, the purpose of the Red Army was to defend Communist Russia's borders and protect changes brought about by the Russian Revolution.

they had been told they were to be **deloused.**[6] The whole transport exactly filled the mortuary to capacity. The doors were then sealed and the gas shaken down through the holes in the roof. I do not know how long this killing took. For a little while a humming sound could be heard. When the powder was thrown in, there were cries of "Gas!," then a great bellowing, and the trapped prisoners hurled themselves against both the doors. But the doors held. They were opened several hours later, so that the place might be aired. It was then that I saw, for the first time, gassed bodies in the mass.

It made me feel uncomfortable and I shuddered, although I had imagined that death by gassing would be worse than it was. I had always thought that the victims would experience a terrible choking sensation. But the bodies, without exception, showed no signs of convulsion. The doctors explained to me that the prussic acid had a paralyzing effect on the lungs, but its action was so quick and strong that death came before the convulsions could set in, and in this its effects differed from those produced by carbon monoxide or by a general oxygen deficiency.

The killing of these Russian prisoners-of-war did not cause me much concern at the time. The order had been given, and I had to carry it out. I must even admit that this gassing set my mind at rest, for the mass extermination of the Jews was to start soon and at that time neither Eichmann nor I was certain how these mass killings were to be carried out. It would be by gas, but we did not know which gas or how it was to be used. Now we had the gas, and we had established a procedure. I always shuddered at the prospect of carrying out exterminations by shooting, when I thought of the vast numbers concerned, and of the women and children. The shooting of hostages, and the group executions ordered by the Reichsführer SS or by the Reich Security

---

[6] **deloused**—rid of lice.

Head Office had been enough for me. I was therefore relieved to think that we were to be spared all these blood-baths, and that the victims too would be spared suffering until their last moment came. It was precisely this which had caused me the greatest concern when I had heard Eichmann's description of Jews being mown down by the Special Squads armed with machine-guns and machine-pistols. Many gruesome scenes are said to have taken place, people running away after being shot, the finishing off of the wounded and particularly of the women and children. Many members of the *Einsatzkommandos,* unable to endure wading through blood any longer, had committed suicide. Some had even gone mad. Most of the members of these *Kommandos* had to rely on alcohol when carrying out their horrible work. According to Höfle's description, the men employed at Globocnik's extermination centers consumed amazing quantities of alcohol. . . .

This mass extermination, with all its attendant circumstances, did not, as I know, fail to affect those who took a part in it. With very few exceptions, nearly all of those detailed to do this monstrous "work," this "service," and who, like myself, have given sufficient thought to the matter, have been deeply marked by these events.

Many of the men involved approached me as I went my rounds through the extermination buildings, and poured out their anxieties and impressions to me, in the hope that I could allay them.

Again and again during these confidential conversations I was asked: is it necessary that we do all this? Is it necessary that hundreds of thousands of women and children be destroyed? And I, who in my innermost being had on countless occasions asked myself exactly this question, could only fob them off and attempt to console them by repeating that it was done on Hitler's order. I had to tell them that this extermination of Jewry had to be, so that Germany and our posterity might be freed for ever from their relentless adversaries.

There was no doubt in the mind of any of us that Hitler's order had to be obeyed regardless, and that it was the duty of the SS to carry it out. Nevertheless we were all tormented by secret doubts.

I myself dared not admit to such doubts. In order to make my subordinates carry on with their task, it was psychologically essential that I myself appear convinced of the necessity for this gruesomely harsh order.

Everyone watched me. They observed the impression produced upon me by the kind of scenes that I have described above, and my reactions. Every word I said on the subject was discussed. I had to exercise intense self-control in order to prevent my innermost doubts and feelings of oppression from becoming apparent.

I had to appear cold and indifferent to events that must have wrung the heart of anyone possessed of human feelings. I might not even look away when afraid lest my natural emotions got the upper hand. I had to watch coldly, while the mothers with laughing or crying children went into the gas-chambers.

On one occasion two small children were so absorbed in some game that they quite refused to let their mother tear them away from it. Even the Jews of the Special Detachment were reluctant to pick the children up. The imploring look in the eyes of the mother, who certainly knew what was happening, is something I shall never forget. The people were already in the gas-chamber and becoming restive, and I had to act. Everyone was looking at me. I nodded to the junior non-commissioned officer on duty and he picked up the screaming, struggling children in his arms and carried them into the gas-chamber, accompanied by their mother who was weeping in the most heart-rending fashion.

My pity was so great that I longed to vanish from the scene: yet I might not show the slightest trace of emotion.

I had to see everything. I had to watch hour after hour, by day and by night, the removal and burning of the bodies, the extraction of the teeth, the cutting of the hair, the whole grisly, interminable business. I had to stand for hours on end in the ghastly stench, while the mass graves were being opened and the bodies dragged out and burned.

I had to look through the peep-hole of the gas-chambers and watch the process of death itself, because the doctors wanted me to see it.

I had to do all this because I was the one to whom everyone looked, because I had to show them all that I did not merely issue the orders and make the regulations but was also prepared myself to be present at whatever task I had assigned to my subordinates.

The Reichsführer SS sent various high-ranking Party leaders and SS officers to Auschwitz so that they might see for themselves the process of extermination of the Jews. They were all deeply impressed by what they saw. Some who had previously spoken most loudly about the necessity for this extermination fell silent once they had actually seen the "final solution of the Jewish problem." I was repeatedly asked how I and my men could go on watching these operations, and how we were able to stand it.

My invariable answer was that the iron determination with which we must carry out Hitler's orders could only be obtained by a stifling of all human emotions. Each of these gentlemen declared that he was glad the job had not been given to him.

QUESTIONS TO CONSIDER

1. What "excuse" does Höss offer for his participation in building the camp at Auschwitz?

2. What is Höss's attitude toward gassing the Jews? Why was this action appealing to him?

3. What methods did Höss use to cope with watching thousands of people die? How did his "job" affect his daily life?

Liberation

Liberation[1]

BY LUCILLE EICHENGREEN

Early in 1945, the Allied and Soviet armies were pushing quickly toward Germany and the concentration camps were one by one being evacuated as they came under threat of liberation. The Germans forced the surviving prisoners into death marches from one camp to another. But, slowly, the Holocaust was coming to an end. Allied and Soviet troops were appalled by what they found in the camps they liberated. Pictures of the camps began to circulate in the West and a wave of revulsion struck the outside world. Lucille Eichengreen was a German Jew born in 1925. She survived internment at Auschwitz and Bergen-Belsen, from which she was liberated in 1945. Eichengreen's parents and sister Karin died in the Holocaust. The following account of the liberation of Bergen-Belsen is taken from Eichengreen's book From Ashes to Life: My Memories of the Holocaust *(1994).*

It was an unusually quiet morning. The sky was overcast. The guard towers were manned, and as usual,

---

[1] **liberation**—being set free.

the SS[2] kept their machine guns aimed at us. But something was different . . . odd. Although the SS wore their usual uniforms, they had added white armbands. We wondered what it might mean.

At noon Elli and I stood outside the barracks, the sun straight overhead. Suddenly, the ground trembled beneath our feet, and a rumbling noise filled the air. Cautiously, we ventured toward the middle of the compound, then closer to the barbed wire that separated us from the main camp road. There, we saw tanks—huge, crawling monsters beginning to line the street from end to end.

The men on top of the tanks wore khaki uniforms. We watched, stunned and bewildered. A woman's shrill, hysterical cry pierced the air as she pointed to the soldiers, "Look, they're British . . . They've come, the war must be over! We are free!"

We watched with both fear and disbelief. Could it be true? We stood motionless until the soldiers jumped off the tanks and walked toward the camp gate. Some of us began to cry, others cheered and laughed as several uniformed British officers entered the camp. The Germans seemed suddenly to have disappeared. The women pressed against the fence and the gate, now guarded by the soldiers in khaki. We followed their every gesture, still not sure that these were our liberators.

Finally, one of them spoke to us in English. "We have liberated this camp. But we are not prepared for what we have found and seen with our own eyes. We'll try to rush in food, water, and medical supplies."

So it was true. We were liberated—finally! Tears, laughter, hugging, and uncontrollable senseless screams burst out of us. The British watched in silence, staring at us, their eyes reflecting horror and disbelief. When we

---

[2] SS—Nazis who served as Hitler's bodyguard and as a policing unit of the German army.

calmed down, the same soldier asked if anyone understood English.

Along with several others, I raised my hand.

"Good, we can use you. We need you to translate for us." They watched us carefully. They looked at our torn, filthy clothing and our thin faces, stained with tears. We saw the troubled bewilderment in their eyes.

I was immediately assigned to three officers. The tall one introduced himself. "I'm Major Brinton. I'm from Scotland. You'll get used to my accent," he laughed. "I'd like to see the inside of several barracks, talk to people, and ask some questions. You'll translate for me."

With more energy than I thought I could muster, I led the way. We walked into the nearest barracks building. Most of the women there had been too weak to come out; some were on the verge of death. The major asked for names, nationalities, and how long they had been in the camps. Most inmates cried; some tried to kiss the hands of the officers. All of them begged for food. I looked at the British. There was horror in their faces. They were unable to comprehend what they saw. They stared at human beings who were barely human, reduced to skeletons with burning eyes and halting voices, bearing little resemblance to women. These still-breathing collections of bones all hoped to live. Their hollow eyes followed us.

The compound housing the men was even worse. I had never been there before. These men had been in Bergen-Belsen a long time; they no longer talked or smiled. On a corner bunk, we saw a skeleton of a man, so emaciated that his skull showed every bone. He stared at us through sunken, feverishly blank, burning eyes. He held a knife in one hand, and as we watched, he slashed away at the thigh of a nearby corpse and then hungrily devoured the flesh. Two of the three officers turned and ran; the third vomited where he stood.

One of the officers screamed, "For Christ's sake, let's get some help!"

I was paralyzed. I had seen and experienced much, but this man left me shaken. What had we become? The Germans had succeeded in reducing us to subhumans. Would we ever be normal again? It seemed impossible. Despite our liberation, I was totally without hope.

The British were quiet. They had seen more than they had bargained for. "Enough for today. Come to the camp gate tomorrow morning at 8:00," they said to me, "and we'll see where we can use you."

The major pressed a small packet of biscuits and several cigarettes into my hand.

"Thank you," I murmured.

"Don't mention it," he sadly replied.

It was late when I returned to our barracks. Elli and I sat on the floor and shared the biscuits and cigarettes. We were silent, still too numb to comprehend all that had happened. Sleep was impossible. My mind raced with plans for the future. I'd have to write to my family in Palestine, in England, and in the United States. They had not heard from any of us in more than four years. They did not know that Mother and Father had been murdered. And Karin—where was she now? I could only wonder and hope. Maybe I would hear from her . . . maybe she would come to Hamburg . . . maybe . . . I thought about our separation during the selection in the Lodz ghetto. Where had they taken her? Had she been liberated, too?

Even though liberation seemed to promise a return to a normal life, it did not bring happiness. Instead, it revived feelings that had long been numbed by the daily struggle for both mental and physical survival—feelings of guilt, loneliness, and utter devastation. The reality of liberation was so different from what I had imagined. I had dreamed of a great party, with fanfare, music, dancing, and fireworks. There was, however, only renewed sorrow for the dead and little hope for the living. Liberation had come quietly, and it had brought with it the realization that thousands of us had not lived to see this moment. Many of us would not live even until the end of the week.

It was almost midnight when the British troops managed to bring drinking water into the camp. This was followed by a huge supply of two-pound tins filled with pieces of pork and lard. Most of the former inmates gulped down the contents of the entire can in minutes. I still chewed on my biscuits, afraid to touch the pork. Within less than an hour, those who had eaten the pork were vomiting and writhing with stomach cramps. Elli and I walked outside; the smell inside the barracks had become more unbearable than ever. I decided to beg the British for more biscuits or bread until our stomachs could get used to food again.

As dawn broke the next morning, the five of us chosen to translate already stood at the gate. Finally, as the sun appeared on the horizon, the major and several officers arrived. The major wanted to know how long we had been waiting. When we told him, "Since daybreak," he looked perplexed. We explained that we had no watches, that they had been taken by the Germans in Auschwitz.

"Come with me," said the major.

For the first time since my arrival at Bergen-Belsen, the camp gate was opened for us, and we walked through it. We had never before left the confines of the camp, and walking into the former SS area without a single German confronting us seemed unbelievable.

We followed the major to the German barracks and stopped in front of a green building marked "Supplies." Inside, on tables, benches, and the floor were hundreds of boxes, neatly sorted and filled with ladies' watches, men's watches, rings, bracelets, brooches, and strings of pearls. Along the far wall were huge boxes filled to the brim with gold coins and foreign currency. We stared in stunned silence, reluctantly remembering Auschwitz and how these heirlooms had been torn from our arms, fingers, and necks. Piles of gold teeth, removed from the mouths of the dead, were hoarded here, destined for distribution or sale to Germans.

"I want each of you to choose a watch so you can be on time for work. Just make sure it still runs," the major said, rather matter-of-factly.

I stretched out my hand, only to pull it back. I wondered about the owners. I could still see the faces of my fellow prisoners as they stood huddled, fearing the worst. Where were they now? Major Brinton's voice ended my ruminations: "Come on, make up your mind!"

I picked up a small, oblong silver watch, wound it, and saw the second hand move. Unbelievable! The back of the watch was slightly rusty, the leather strap black and worn. I put the watch around my wrist with a silent prayer that its owner was alive and that someday she would recognize the watch and claim it. She never did.

Several days after liberation, life at Bergen-Belsen started to take on a certain routine. My work as an interpreter kept me busy, and I momentarily forgot everything else. Food improved; there was hot stew now, dark bread, hot tea. No one went hungry. Still, hundreds died daily. For them, food and freedom had come too late.

Two weeks after I began working, I summoned enough courage to ask the major if I could shower or bathe. He looked at me, embarrassed. How could he understand? It had been almost four years.

"Of course. I'll make arrangements for you and the others," he said.

A young woman officer of the British Red Cross took the five of us to the showers in the former SS barracks. We were handed a small piece of soap and a towel. The showers worked! Hot water streamed over our cropped hair and thin bodies. It was heaven. I soaped and rinsed again and then again, hoping that perhaps the clean, hot water would put distance between the dark, bloody past and the present. But it didn't work. The past could not be forgotten, not then— perhaps not ever. I finally stepped outside, dried myself, and put on my ragged, dirty clothing. In time perhaps we would have new, clean clothes.

During the days that followed, huge bulldozers were brought into the camp. They dug deep craters. Then they shoveled the thousands of dead bodies that lay in a heap into the gaping pit. Those who could attended the services. I stood at the rim of the pit, listening to the army chaplain recite prayers in English and the Kaddish in Hebrew. Suddenly the earth heaved, my head spun, my arms flailed, and the world around me turned black.

Later, when I opened my eyes, I found myself in a light, airy room. A kind voice told me that I had fainted. Gentle hands were applying cool compresses to my head, and I burst into uncontrollable sobs. I could neither talk nor explain; no words could sound the depths of my pain and sorrow or articulate the agony of total loss.

QUESTIONS TO CONSIDER

1. How did the British officers feel when they liberated the camp? What do you think they had expected to see?

2. What had the narrator expected liberation to be like? Compare and contrast the expectations of liberation with reality.

3. What was the significance of the narrator's shower?

from

Night

BY ELIE WIESEL

Elie Wiesel won the Nobel Peace Prize in 1986 for his efforts to commemorate the victims of the Holocaust. Wiesel has written more than thirty books, many of which are part of an attempt to come to terms with his experiences in the Holocaust and convince other survivors that they should bear no guilt for surviving when so many others died. Wiesel (1928–) is a Romanian Jew, who, along with his entire community of 15,000 Jews, was deported to Auschwitz in 1944. One of his sisters and his mother were immediately gassed, while his father, two elder sisters, and Elie were put to work as slave laborers. Wiesel's father died after he and his son were moved to Buchenwald. After liberation, Wiesel went to France, where he completed his education and became a journalist. Ten years after his liberation, he began to try and write about his experiences at Auschwitz and Buchenwald. The following excerpt from his acclaimed work Night *(1958) describes how he felt after liberation.*

I had to stay at Buchenwald[1] until April eleventh. I have nothing to say of my life during this period. It no longer mattered. After my father's death, nothing could touch me any more.

I was transferred to the children's block, where there were six hundred of us.

The front[2] was drawing nearer.

I spent my days in a state of total idleness. And I had but one desire—to eat. I no longer thought of my father or of my mother.

From time to time I would dream of a drop of soup, of an extra ration of soup.

On April fifth, the wheel of history turned.

It was late in the afternoon. We were standing in the block, waiting for an SS man to come and count us. He was late in coming. Such a delay was unknown till then in the history of Buchenwald. Something must have happened.

Two hours later the loudspeakers sent out an order from the head of the camp: all Jews must come to the assembly place.

This was the end! Hitler was going to keep his promise.

The children in our block went toward the place. There was nothing else we could do. Gustav, the head of the block, made this clear to us with his **truncheon.**[3] But on the way we met some prisoners who whispered to us:

"Go back to your block. The Germans are going to shoot you. Go back to your block, and don't move."

We went back to our block. We learned on the way that the camp resistance organization had decided not to abandon the Jews and was going to prevent their being liquidated.

---

[1] Buchenwald—village in central Germany, site of a Nazi concentration camp.
[2] front—battlefront.
[3] **truncheon**—a stick cut and shaped for use as a weapon; club.

As it was late and there was great upheaval—innumerable Jews had passed themselves off as non-Jews—the head of the camp decided that a general roll call would take place the following day. Everybody would have to be present.

The roll call took place. The head of the camp announced that Buchenwald was to be liquidated. Ten blocks of deportees would be evacuated each day. From this moment, there would be no further distribution of bread and soup. And the evacuation began. Every day, several thousand prisoners went through the camp gate and never came back.

On April tenth, there were still about twenty thousand of us in the camp, including several hundred children. They decided to evacuate us all at once, right on until the evening. Afterward, they were going to blow up the camp.

So we were massed in the huge assembly square, in rows of five, waiting to see the gate open. Suddenly, the sirens began to wail. An alert! We went back to the blocks. It was too late to evacuate us that evening. The evacuation was postponed again to the following day.

We were tormented with hunger. We had eaten nothing for six days, except a bit of grass or some potato peelings found near the kitchens.

At ten o'clock in the morning the SS scattered through the camp, moving the last victims toward the assembly place.

Then the resistance movement decided to act. Armed men suddenly rose up everywhere. Bursts of firing. Grenades exploding. We children stayed flat on the ground in the block.

The battle did not last long. Toward noon everything was quiet again. The SS had fled and the resistance had taken charge of the running of the camp.

At about six o'clock in the evening, the first American tank stood at the gates of Buchenwald.

Our first act as free men was to throw ourselves onto the provisions. We thought only of that. Not of revenge, not of our families. Nothing but bread.

And even when we were no longer hungry, there was still no one who thought of revenge. On the following day, some of the young men went to Weimar to get some potatoes and clothes—and to sleep with girls. But of revenge, not a sign.

Three days after the **liberation**[4] of Buchenwald I became very ill with food poisoning. I was transferred to the hospital and spent two weeks between life and death.

One day I was able to get up, after gathering all my strength. I wanted to see myself in the mirror hanging on the opposite wall. I had not seen myself since the ghetto.

From the depths of the mirror, a corpse gazed back at me.

The look in his eyes, as they stared into mine, has never left me.

---

[4] **liberation**—being set free.

QUESTIONS TO CONSIDER

1. Wiesel says that "even when we were no longer hungry, there was still no one who thought of revenge." Why do you think this was true?

2. Wiesel describes his bout with food poisoning. What is ironic about his illness?

3. What does Wiesel see when he looks in the mirror? What effect does this sight have on him?

Poems of Liberation

The idea of liberation is of great importance to the imprisoned. All those sent to a concentration camp dreamed of freedom. The Italian writer Primo Levi has written at length on how survivors reacted to their freedom when it came (see "Shame" page 172). Abraham Sutzkever (see biography on page 74) wrote the poem "How" wondering how he would act after surviving the horror of the Vilna ghetto. Nelly Sachs (see biography on page 191), who was spared the horrors of being a Jew in Nazi Germany by emigrating to Sweden, imagined the feelings of the liberated in her poem "Chorus of the Rescued."

Chorus of the Rescued

BY NELLY SACHS

We, the rescued,
From whose hollow bones death had begun to whittle
    his flutes,

And on whose sinews he had already stroked his bow—
Our bodies continue to **lament**[1]
With their **mutilated**[2] music.
We, the rescued,
The nooses wound for our necks still dangle
before us in the blue air—
Hourglasses still fill with our dripping blood.
We, the rescued,
The worms of fear still feed on us.
Our constellation is buried in dust.
We, the rescued,
Beg you:
Show us your sun, but gradually.
Lead us from star to star, step by step.
Be gentle when you teach us to live again.
Lest the song of a bird,
Or a pail being filled at the well,
Let our badly sealed pain burst forth again
and carry us away—
We beg you:
Do not show us an angry dog, not yet—
It could be, it could be
That we will dissolve into dust—
Dissolve into dust before your eyes.
For what binds our fabric together?
We whose breath vacated us,
Whose soul fled to Him out of that midnight
Long before our bodies were rescued
Into the ark of the moment.
We, the rescued,
We press your hand
We look into your eye—
But all that binds us together now is leave-taking,
The leave-taking in the dust
Binds us together with you.

---

[1] **lament**—a crying out in grief.

[2] **mutilated**—maimed; made imperfect.

How?

BY ABRAHAM SUTZKEVER

How and with what will you fill
Your goblet on the day of Liberation?
In your joy, are you ready to feel
The dark scream of your past
Where skulls of days **congeal**[3]
In a bottomless pit?

You will look for a key to fit
Your jammed locks.
Like bread you will bite the streets
And think: better the past.
And time will drill you quietly
Like a cricket caught in a fist.

And your memory will be like
An old buried city.
Your eternal gaze will crawl
Like a mole, like a mole—

Vilna Ghetto, February 14, 1943

---

[3] **congeal**—solidify; curdle.

QUESTIONS TO CONSIDER

1. What message or feeling do each of the poems convey about liberation?

2. Do the poems have similar or different tones? How does the tone of these poems compare to the tone you would expect in a poem about liberation?

Liberated prisoners at Dachau.

Prisoners at Dachau wildly cheering the arrival of the American army.
Most of them had been scheduled to be gassed on the day the American
troops arrived.
▼

Liberation

Liberated prisoners at Ebensee camp in Austria, where survivors of other camps had been marched as the Allied armies drew closer to camps such as Mauthausen.

▼

At the Guson concentration camp in Austria, women prisoners are being freed.

▲

To punish the Germans, Americans forced German civilians to hold burials for victims who were murdered by the SS troops. Civilians said that the SS ordered them to remain in their homes while the SS brutally murdered victims in the camps.

Civilians near Landsberg transport bodies of victims murdered at the camp. ▶

▲

German women and men of Nounburg carry bodies of victims of the camps to a burial site to give the victims a decent burial place.

▲

Seeking Justice Here a Russian slave laborer held in Torneau points out one of the former Nazi guards who brutally beat prisoners.

At the Nuremberg war crimes trial, seven of the twenty-three defendants sit listening to evidence presented against them. The defendants were all members of Hitler's extermination SS units.

▼

Responding to
the Holocaust

Shame

BY PRIMO LEVI

Primo Levi (1919–1987) was a Jewish chemist who took an active part in the resistance in Italy. In 1943 he was captured by the Germans and sent to Auschwitz. Levi survived and after the war began to write about his experience as a form of "interior libera- tion." His book, If This Be a Man *(1947), is the first in a trilogy of memoirs which recount his time in Auschwitz and liberation. The trilogy, which includes* The Reawakening *(1963) and* The Periodic Table *(1975), is distinguished by the detachment of the writing and the literary reflections on what is a very personal horror. Levi also wrote widely about the meaning of the Holocaust and how it shaped a survivor's life. "Shame" examines why survivors suffered so deeply from that emotion.*

A certain fixed image has been proposed innumer- able times, consecrated by literature and poetry, and picked up by the cinema: "the quiet after the storm," when all hearts rejoice. "To be freed from pain/is delight- ful for us." The disease runs its course and health returns. To deliver us from imprisonment "our boys," the liberators, arrive just in time, with waving flags; the soldier returns and again finds his family and peace.

Judging by the stories told by many who came back and from my own memories, Leopardi[1] the pessimist stretched the truth in this representation; despite himself, he showed himself to be an optimist. In the majority of cases, the hour of liberation was neither joyful nor lighthearted. For most it occurred against a tragic background of destruction, slaughter, and suffering. Just as they felt they were again becoming men, that is, responsible, the sorrows of men returned: the sorrow of the dispersed or lost family; the universal suffering all around; their own exhaustion, which seemed definitive, past cure; the problems of a life to begin all over again amid the rubble, often alone. Not "pleasure the son of misery," but misery the son of misery. Leaving pain behind was a delight for only a few fortunate beings, or only for a few instants, or for very simple souls; almost always it coincided with a phase of anguish.

Anguish is known to everyone, even children, and everyone knows that it is often blank, undifferentiated. Rarely does it carry a clearly written label that also contains its motivation; any label it does have is often **mendacious.**[2] One can believe or declare oneself to be anguished for one reason and be so due to something totally different. One can think that one is suffering at facing the future and instead be suffering because of one's past; one can think that one is suffering for others, out of pity, out of compassion, and instead be suffering for one's own reasons, more or less profound, more or less avowable and avowed, sometimes so deep that only the specialist, the analyst of souls, knows how to exhume them.

Naturally, I dare not maintain that the movie script I referred to before is false in every case. Many liberations

---

[1] Leopardi, Giacomo (1798–1837)—Italian lyric poet, noted for his melancholy view of a world utterly against mankind.

[2] **mendacious**—lying; untruthful.

were experienced with full, authentic joy—above all by combatants, both military and political, who at that moment saw the aspirations of their militancy and their lives realized, and also on the part of those who had suffered less and for less time, or only in their own person and not because of their family, friends, or loved ones. And besides, luckily, human beings are not all the same. There are among us those who have the virtue and the privilege of extracting, isolating those instants of happiness, of enjoying them fully, as though they were extracting pure gold from dross. And finally, among the testimonies, written or spoken, some are unconsciously stylized, in which convention prevails over genuine memory: "Whoever is freed from slavery rejoices. I too was liberated, hence I too rejoice over it. In all films, all novels, just as in *Fidelio*,[3] the shattering of the chains is a moment of solemn or fervid jubilation, and so was mine." This is a specific case of that drifting of memory . . . which is accentuated with the passing of years and the piling up of the experiences of others, true or presumed, on one's own. But anyone who, purportedly or by temperament, shuns rhetoric, usually speaks in a different voice. This, for example, is how, on the last page of his memoir, *Eyewitness Auschwitz: Three Years in the Gas Chambers,* Filip Müller, whose experience was much more terrible than mine, describes his liberation:

> Although it may seem incredible, I had a complete letdown or depression. That moment, on which for three years all my thoughts and secret desires were concentrated, did not awaken happiness or any other feeling in me. I let myself fall from my pallet and crawled to the door. Once outside I tried vainly to go further, then I simply lay down on the ground in the woods and fell asleep.

---

[3] *Fidelio*—opera by Beethoven, at the end of which the title character is released from prison and sings a famous aria in praise of freedom.

I now reread the passage from my own book, *The Reawakening*, which was published in Italy only in 1963, although I had written these words as early as 1947. In it is a description of the first Russian soldiers facing our Lager[4] packed with corpses and dying prisoners.

> They did not greet us, nor smile; they seemed oppressed, not only by pity but also by a confused restraint which sealed their mouths, and kept their eyes fastened on the funereal scene. It was the same shame which we knew so well, which submerged us after the selections, and every time we had to witness or undergo an outrage: the shame that the Germans never knew, the shame which the just man experiences when confronted by a crime committed by another, and he feels remorse because of its existence, because of its having been irrevocably introduced into the world of existing things, and because his will has proven nonexistent or feeble and was incapable of putting up a good defense.

I do not think that there is anything I need erase or correct, but there is something I must add. That many (including me) experienced "shame," that is, a feeling of guilt during the imprisonment and afterward, is an ascertained fact confirmed by numerous testimonies. It may seem absurd, but it is a fact. I will try to interpret it myself and to comment on the interpretations of others.

As I mentioned at the start, the vague discomfort which accompanied liberation was not precisely shame, but it was perceived as such. Why? There are various possible explanations.

In my opinion, the feeling of shame or guilt that coincided with reacquired freedom was extremely composite: it contained diverse elements, and in diverse

---

[4] Lager—unit in which prisoners were grouped and housed.

proportions for each individual. It must be remembered that each of us, both objectively and subjectively, lived the Lager in his own way.

Coming out of the darkness, one suffered because of the reacquired consciousness of having been diminished. Not by our will, cowardice, or fault, yet nevertheless we had lived for months and years at an animal level: our days had been encumbered from dawn to dusk by hunger, fatigue, cold, and fear, and any space for reflection, reasoning, experiencing emotions was wiped out. We endured filth, promiscuity, and destitution, suffering much less than we would have suffered from such things in normal life, because our moral yardstick had changed. Furthermore, all of us had stolen: in the kitchen, the factory, the camp, in short, "from the others," from the opposing side, but it was theft nevertheless. Some (few) had fallen so low as to steal bread from their own companions. We had not only forgotten our country and our culture, but also our family, our past, the future we had imagined for ourselves, because, like animals, we were confined to the present moment. Only at rare intervals did we come out of this condition of leveling, during the very few Sundays of rest, the fleeting minutes before falling asleep, or the fury of the air raids, but these were painful moments precisely because they gave us the opportunity to measure our diminishment from the outside.

I believe that it was precisely this turning to look back at the "perilous water" that gave rise to so many suicides after (sometimes immediately after) Liberation. It was in any case a critical moment which coincided with a flood of rethinking and depression. By contrast, all historians of the Lager—and also of the Soviet camps—agree in pointing out that cases of suicide *during* imprisonment were rare. Several explanations of this fact have been put forward; for my part I offer three, which are not mutually exclusive.

First of all, suicide is an act of man and not of the animal. It is a meditated act, a noninstinctive, unnatural choice, and in the Lager there were few opportunities to choose: people lived precisely like enslaved animals that sometimes let themselves die but do not kill themselves.

Secondly, "there were other things to think about," as the saying goes. The day was dense: one had to think about satisfying hunger, in some way elude fatigue and cold, avoid the blows. Precisely because of the constant imminence of death there was no time to concentrate on the idea of death. Svevo's[5] remark in *Confessions of Zeno*, when he ruthlessly describes his father's agony, has the rawness of truth: "When one is dying, one is much too busy to think about death. All one's organism is devoted to breathing."

Thirdly, in the majority of cases, suicide is born from a feeling of guilt that no punishment has **attenuated;** [6] now, the harshness of imprisonment was perceived as punishment, and the feeling of guilt (if there is punishment, there must have been guilt) was relegated to the background, only to re-emerge after the Liberation. In other words, there was no need to punish oneself by suicide because of a (true or presumed) guilt: one was already **expiating**[7] it by one's daily suffering.

What guilt? When all was over, the awareness emerged that we had not done anything, or not enough, against the system into which we had been absorbed. About the failed resistance in the Lagers, or, more accurately, in some Lagers, too much has been said, too superficially, above all by people who had altogether different crimes to account for. Anyone who made the attempt knows that there existed situations, collective

---

[5] Svevo, Italo (1861–1928)—Italian novelist; his most famous work is the analytical *Confessions of Zeno*.

[6] **attenuated**—weakened; reduced.

[7] **expiating**—making amends for a wrong or a sin.

or personal, in which active resistance was possible, and others, much more frequent, in which it was not. It is known that, especially in 1941, millions of Soviet military prisoners fell into German hands. They were young, generally well nourished and robust; they had military and political training, and often they formed organic units with soldiers with the rank of corporal and up, noncommissioned officers, and officers. They hated the Germans who had invaded their country, and yet they rarely resisted. Malnutrition, despoilment, and other physical discomforts, which it is so easy and economically advantageous to provoke and at which the Nazis were masters, are rapidly destructive and paralyze before destroying, all the more so when they are preceded by years of segregation, humiliation, maltreatment, forced migration, laceration of family ties, rupture of contact with the rest of the world—that is to say, the situation of the bulk of the prisoners who had landed in Auschwitz after the introductory hell of the ghettos or the collection camps.

Therefore, on a rational plane, there should not have been much to be ashamed of, but shame persisted nevertheless, especially for the few bright examples of those who had the strength and possibility to resist. I spoke about this in the chapter "The Last" in *Survival in Auschwitz*, where I described the public hanging of a resistor before a terrified and apathetic crowd of prisoners. This is a thought that then just barely grazed us, but that returned "afterward": you too could have, you certainly should have. And this is a judgment that the survivor believes he sees in the eyes of those (especially the young) who listen to his stories and judge with facile hindsight, or who perhaps feel cruelly repelled. Consciously or not, he feels accused and judged, compelled to justify and defend himself.

More realistic is self-accusation, or the accusation of having failed in terms of human solidarity. Few survivors feel guilty about having deliberately damaged, robbed, or beaten a companion. Those who did so (the Kapos, but not only they) block out the memory. By contrast, however, almost everybody feels guilty of having omitted to offer help. The presence at your side of a weaker—or less cunning, or older, or too young—companion, hounding you with his demands for help or with his simple presence, in itself an entreaty, is a constant in the life of the Lager. The demand for solidarity, for a human word, advice, even just a listening ear, was permanent and universal but rarely satisfied. There was no time, space, privacy, patience, strength; most often, the person to whom the request was addressed found himself in his turn in a state of need, entitled to comfort.

I remember with a certain relief that I once tried to give courage (at a moment when I felt I had some) to an eighteen-year-old Italian who had just arrived, who was floundering in the bottomless despair of his first days in camp. I forget what I told him, certainly words of hope, perhaps a few lies, acceptable to a "new arrival," expressed with the authority of my twenty-five years and my three months of seniority; at any rate, I made him the gift of a momentary attention. But I also remember, with disquiet, that much more often I shrugged my shoulders impatiently at other requests, and this precisely when I had been in camp for almost a year and so had accumulated a good store of experience: but I had also deeply **assimilated**[8] the principal rule of the place, which made it mandatory that you take care of yourself first of all. I never found this rule expressed with as much frankness as in *Prisoners of Fear* by Ella Lingens-Reiner (where, however, the woman doctor, regardless of her own statement, proved to be generous and brave and saved many lives): "How was I able to

---

[8] **assimilated**—took in and made part of oneself; absorbed.

survive in Auschwitz? My principle is: I come first, second, and third. Then nothing, then again I; and then all the others. . . ."

* * *

Are you ashamed because you are alive in place of another? And in particular, of a man more generous, more sensitive, more useful, wiser, worthier of living than you? You cannot block out such feelings: you examine yourself, you review your memories, hoping to find them all, and that none of them are masked or disguised. No, you find no obvious **transgressions,**[9] you did not usurp anyone's place, you did not beat anyone (but would you have had the strength to do so?), you did not accept positions (but none were offered to you . . .), you did not steal anyone's bread; nevertheless you cannot exclude it. It is no more than a supposition, indeed the shadow of a suspicion: that each man is his brother's Cain,[10] that each one of us (but this time I say "us" in a much vaster, indeed, universal sense) has usurped his neighbor's place and lived in his stead. It is a supposition, but it gnaws at us; it has nestled deeply like a woodworm; although unseen from the outside, it gnaws and rasps.

After my return from imprisonment I was visited by a friend older than myself, mild and **intransigent,**[11] the cultivator of a personal religion, which, however, always seemed to me severe and serious. He was glad to find me alive and basically unhurt, perhaps matured and fortified, certainly enriched. He told me that my having survived could not be the work of chance, of an accumulation of fortunate circumstances (as I did then

---

[9] **transgressions**—breaking laws or commands.

[10] Cain—in the Bible, the oldest son of Adam and Eve. He killed his brother Abel. Cain is also used to mean "murderer."

[11] **intransigent**—unwilling to agree or compromise.

and still do maintain) but rather of Providence. I bore the mark, I was an elect: I, the nonbeliever, and even less of a believer after the season of Auschwitz, was a person touched by Grace, a saved man. And why me? It is impossible to know, he answered. Perhaps because I had to write, and by writing bear witness: Wasn't I in fact then, in 1946, writing a book about my imprisonment?

Such an opinion seemed monstrous to me. It pained me as when one touches an exposed nerve, and kindled the doubt I spoke of before: I might be alive in the place of another, at the expense of another; I might have usurped, that is, in fact, killed. The "saved" of the Lager were not the best, those predestined to do good, the bearers of a message: what I had seen and lived through proved the exact contrary. Preferably the worst survived, the selfish, the violent, the insensitive, the collaborators of the "gray zone," the spies. It was not a certain rule (there were none, nor are there certain rules in human matters), but it was nevertheless a rule. I felt innocent, yes, but enrolled among the saved and therefore in permanent search of a justification in my own eyes and those of others. The worst survived, that is, the fittest; the best all died.

Chaim died, a watchmaker from Krakow, a pious Jew who despite the language difficulties made an effort to understand and be understood, and explained to me, the foreigner, the essential rules for survival during the crucial days of captivity; Szabo died, the **taciturn**[12] Hungarian peasant who was almost two meters tall and so was the hungriest of all, and yet, as long as he had the strength, did not hesitate to help his weaker companions to pull and push; and Robert, a professor at the Sorbonne who spread courage and trust all around him, spoke five languages, wore himself out recording

---

[12] **taciturn**—speaking very little; not fond of talking.

everything in his prodigious memory, and had he lived would have answered the questions which I do not know how to answer; and Baruch died, a longshoreman from Livorno, immediately, on the first day, because he had answered the first punch he had received with punches and was massacred by three Kapos in coalition. These, and innumerable others, died not despite their valor but because of it.

My religious friend had told me that I survived so that I could bear witness. I have done so, as best I could, and I also could not have done so; and I am still doing so, whenever the opportunity presents itself; but the thought that this testifying of mine could by itself gain for me the privilege of surviving and living for many years without serious problems troubles me because I cannot see any proportion between the privilege and its outcome.

I must repeat: we, the survivors, are not the true witnesses. This is an uncomfortable notion of which I have become conscious little by little, reading the memoirs of others and reading mine at a distance of years. We survivors are not only an **exiguous**[13] but also an **anomalous**[14] minority: we are those who by their prevarications or abilities or good luck did not touch bottom. Those who did so, those who saw the Gorgon,[15] have not returned to tell about it or have returned mute, but they are the "Muslims," the submerged, the complete witnesses, the ones whose deposition would have a general significance. They are the rule, we are the exception. Under another sky, and returned from a similar and diverse slavery, Solzhenitsyn[16] also noted:

---

[13] **exiguous**—extremely small.

[14] **anomalous**—irregular; abnormal.

[15] Gorgon—monster of classical mythology, whose face was so frightening that those who looked upon it were turned to stone.

[16] Solzhenitsyn, Aleksandr (1918–), Russian novelist and Nobel-prize winner; he survived the infamous Soviet Gulags and his novels eloquently document the horror of another totalitarian regime.

"Almost all those who served a long sentence and whom you congratulate because they are survivors are unquestionably *pridurki* or were such during the greater part of their imprisonment. Because Lagers are meant for extermination, this should not be forgotten."

In the language of that other concentrationary universe, the *pridurki* are the prisoners who, in one way or another, won a position of privilege, those we called the Prominent.

We who were favored by fate tried, with more or less wisdom, to recount not only our fate but also that of the others, indeed of the drowned; but this was a discourse "on behalf of third parties," the story of things seen at close hand, not experienced personally. The destruction brought to an end, the job completed, was not told by anyone, just as no one ever returned to describe his own death. Even if they had paper and pen, the drowned would not have testified because their death had begun before that of their body. Weeks and months before being snuffed out, they had already lost the ability to observe, to remember, to compare and express themselves. We speak in their stead, by proxy.

We are often asked, as if our past conferred a prophetic ability upon us, whether Auschwitz will return: whether, that is, other slaughters will take place, unilateral, systematic, mechanized, willed, at a governmental level, perpetrated upon innocent and defenseless populations and legitimized by the doctrine of contempt. Prophets, to our good fortune, we are not, but something can be said. That a similar tragedy, almost ignored in the West, did take place, in Cambodia,[17] in about 1975. That the German slaughter could be set off—and after that feed on itself—out of a desire for servitude and smallness of soul, thanks to the

---

[17] Cambodia—southeast Asian country, its Khmer Rouge government slaughtered almost a third of the Cambodian population between 1975 and 1979.

concurrence of a number of factors (the state of war, German technological and organizational perfectionism, Hitler's will and inverted charisma, the lack in Germany of solid democratic roots), not very numerous, each of them indispensable but insufficient if taken singly. These factors can occur again and are already recurring in various parts of the world. The convergence again of all of them within ten or twenty years (there is no sense in speaking of a more remote future) is not very likely but also not impossible. In my opinion, a mass slaughter is particularly unlikely in the Western world, Japan, and also the Soviet Union: the Lagers of World War II are still part of the memory of many, on both the popular and governmental levels, and a sort of immunizational defense is at work which amply coincides with the shame of which I have spoken.

As to what might happen in other parts of the world, or later on, it is prudent to suspend judgment. And the nuclear apocalypse, certainly bilateral, probably instantaneous and definitive, is a greater and different horror, strange, new, which stands outside the theme I have chosen.

QUESTIONS TO CONSIDER

1. Filip Müller, speaking of his liberation, said, "Although it may seem incredible, I had a complete letdown or depression." Why do you think Müller felt that way?

2. Why were suicide attempts during imprisonment in the camps rare?

3. According to Levi, what made survivors of the Holocaust feel shame? What philosophy guided the prisoners in terms of their treatment of others?

Another Meaning of the Holocaust

BY BRUNO BETTELHEIM

Bruno Bettelheim (1903–1990) was well-known as a psychologist and educator in the United States. He was born in Vienna, Austria, and studied psychology, specializing in mentally disturbed children. When the Germans annexed Austria in 1938, Bettelheim was interned in a concentration camp, though he was allowed to emigrate to the United States in 1939. From his experience of Nazism, he wrote an influential book on mass movements entitled Individual and Mass Behavior in Extreme Situations. *Throughout his career, Bettelheim returned to the Holocaust in his writings. The following essay "Another Meaning of the Holocaust" examines the motivations of the Jews during the Holocaust.*

To begin with, it was not the hapless victims of the Nazis who named their incomprehensible and totally unmasterable fate the "holocaust." It was the Americans who applied this artificial and highly technical term to the Nazi extermination of the European Jews. But while the event when named as mass murder most foul evokes the most immediate, most powerful revulsion, when it is designated by a rare technical term, we must first in our minds translate it back into emotionally meaningful language. Using technical or specially created terms instead of words from our common vocabulary is one of the best-known and most widely used distancing devices, separating the intellectual from the emotional experience. Talking about "the holocaust" permits us to manage it intellectually where the raw facts, when given their ordinary names, would overwhelm us emotionally—because it was catastrophe beyond comprehension, beyond the limits of our imagination, unless we force ourselves against our desire to extend it to encompass these terrible events.

This linguistic **circumlocution**[1] began while it all was only in the planning stage. Even the Nazis—usually given to grossness in language and action—shied away from facing openly what they were up to and called this vile mass murder "the final solution of the Jewish problem." After all, solving a problem can be made to appear like an honorable enterprise, as long as we are not forced to recognize that the solution we are about to embark on consists of the completely unprovoked, vicious murder of millions of helpless men, women, and children. The Nuremberg judges of these Nazi criminals followed their example of circumlocution by coining a **neologism**[2] out of one Greek and one Latin root: **genocide**.[3] These artificially created technical terms fail to connect with our strongest feelings. The horror of murder is part of our most common human heritage. From earliest infancy on, it arouses violent **abhorrence**[4] in us. Therefore in whatever form it

---

[1] **circumlocution**—a roundabout expression, such as "the wife of your father's brother" rather than "aunt."

[2] **neologism**—use of new words or of old words with new meanings.

[3] **genocide**—the extermination of a cultural or racial group.

[4] **abhorrence**—a feeling of very great hatred.

appears we should give such an act its true designation and not hide it behind polite, erudite terms created out of classical words.

To call this vile mass murder "the holocaust" is not to give it a special name emphasizing its uniqueness which would permit, over time, the word becoming invested with feelings germane to the event it refers to. The correct definition of "holocaust" is "burnt offering." As such, it is part of the language of the **psalmist**,[5] a meaningful word to all who have some acquaintance with the Bible, full of the richest emotional connotations. By using the term "holocaust," entirely false associations are established through conscious and unconscious connotations between the most vicious of mass murders and ancient rituals of a deeply religious nature.

Using a word with such strong unconscious religious connotations when speaking of the murder of millions of Jews robs the victims of this abominable mass murder of the only thing left to them: their uniqueness. Calling the most callous, most brutal, most horrid, most heinous mass murder a burnt offering is a sacrilege, a **profanation**[6] of God and man.

Martyrdom[7] is part of our religious heritage. A martyr, burned at the stake, is a burnt offering to his god. And it is true that after the Jews were **asphyxiated**,[8] the victims' corpses were burned. But I believe we fool ourselves if we think we are honoring the victims of systematic murder by using this term, which has the highest moral connotations. By doing so, we connect for our own psychological reasons what happened in the extermination camps with historical events we deeply

---

[5] **psalmist**—author of psalms, sacred songs.

[6] **profanation**—act of showing contempt or disregard.

[7] **martyrdom**—death or suffering of a martyr, a person who chooses to die or suffer rather than renounce a religious faith.

[8] **asphyxiated**—killed through lack of oxygen or as a result of poisonous gas.

regret, but also greatly admire. We do so because this makes it easier for us to cope; only in doing so we cope with our distorted image of what happened, not with the events the way they did happen.

By calling the victims of the Nazis "martyrs," we falsify their fate. The true meaning of "martyr" is: "One who voluntarily undergoes the penalty of death for refusing to renounce his faith" *(Oxford English Dictionary)*. The Nazis made sure that nobody could mistakenly think that their victims were murdered for their religious beliefs. Renouncing their faith would have saved none of them. Those who had converted to Christianity were gassed, as were those who were atheists, and those who were deeply religious Jews. They did not die for any conviction, and certainly not out of choice.

Millions of Jews were systematically slaughtered, as were untold other "undesirables," not for any convictions of theirs, but only because they stood in the way of the realization of an illusion. They neither died for their convictions, nor were they slaughtered because of their convictions, but only in consequence of the Nazis' delusional belief about what was required to protect the purity of their assumed superior racial endowment, and what they thought necessary to guarantee them the living space they believed they needed and were entitled to. Thus while these millions were slaughtered for an idea, they did not die for one.

Millions—men, women, and children—were processed after they had been utterly brutalized, their humanity destroyed, their clothes torn from their bodies. Naked, they were sorted into those who were destined to be murdered immediately, and those others who had a short-term usefulness as slave labor. But after a brief interval they, too, were to be herded into the same gas chambers into which the others were immediately piled, there to be asphyxiated so that, in their last moments, they could not prevent themselves from fighting each other in vain for a last breath of air.

To call these most wretched victims of a murderous delusion, of destructive drives run rampant, martyrs or a burnt offering is a distortion invented for our comfort, small as it may be. It pretends that this most vicious of mass murders had some deeper meaning; that in some fashion the victims either offered themselves or at least became sacrifices to a higher cause. It robs them of the last recognition which could be theirs, denies them the last dignity we could accord them: to face and accept what their death was all about, not embellishing it for the small psychological relief this may give us.

We could feel so much better if the victims had acted out of choice. For our emotional relief, therefore, we dwell on the tiny minority who did exercise some choice: the resistance fighters of the Warsaw ghetto, for example, and others like them. We are ready to overlook the fact that these people fought back only at a time when everything was lost, when the overwhelming majority of those who had been forced into the ghettos had already been exterminated without resisting. Certainly those few who finally fought for their survival and their convictions, risking and losing their lives in doing so, deserve our admiration; their deeds give us a moral lift. But the more we dwell on these few, the more unfair are we to the memory of the millions who were slaughtered—who gave in, did not fight back—because we deny them the only thing which up to the very end remained uniquely their own: their fate.

QUESTIONS TO CONSIDER

1. The Nazis coined the phrase "the final solution of the Jewish problem." According to Bettelheim, why did they use this term to describe the action they were taking?

2. What is the meaning of the word "holocaust"? What does Bettelheim assert that the use of this word implies?

3. According to Bettelheim, what do many people assume is the underlying reason for the murders of the Jews? What does he say was the actual motivation behind the killings?

Poems of the Holocaust

Nelly Sachs (1891–1970) is a Jewish poet who took the Holocaust as a principal theme. She too escaped the worst horrors of the Holocaust, escaping from Germany to Sweden in 1940. Almost all of her poetry after the war deals with the Holocaust or the extremes of human suffering.

Paul Celan was the pseudonym of the Romanian poet Paul Ancel (1920–1970). Celan, a Jew, escaped deportation by hiding, but both his parents died in the camps. After the war, Celan repeatedly explored the Holocaust in his writings, and his poem "Death Fugue" is arguably the most famous poem written in German in the postwar era.

Jacob Glatstein (1896–1971) was born in Poland, but emigrated to the United States in 1914. He devoted his whole career to writing about Jewish themes. His poems about the Holocaust are powerful reactions to this great crisis.

If I Only Knew

BY NELLY SACHS

If I only knew
On what your last look rested.
Was it a stone that had drunk
So many last looks that they fell
Blindly upon its blindness?

Or was it earth,
Enough to fill a shoe,
And black already
With so much parting
And with so much killing?

Or was it your last road
That brought you a farewell from all the roads
You had walked?

A puddle, a bit of shining metal,
Perhaps the buckle of your enemy's belt,
Or some other small **augury**[1]
Of heaven?

Or did this earth,
Which lets no one depart unloved,
Send you a bird-sign through the air,
Reminding your soul that it quivered
In the torment of its burnt body?

---

[1] **augury**—prediction; sign; omen.

Death Fugue[2]

PAUL CELAN

Black milk of daybreak we drink it at sundown
we drink it at noon in the morning we drink it at
    night
we drink and we drink it
we dig a grave in the breezes there one lies
    unconfined
A man lives in the house he plays with the serpents
    he writes
he writes when dusk falls to Germany your golden
    hair Margarete
he writes it and steps out of doors and the stars are
    flashing he whistles his pack out
he whistles his Jews out in earth has them dig for a
    grave
he commands us strike up for the dance

Black milk of daybreak we drink you at night
we drink in the morning at noon we drink you at
    sundown
we drink and we drink you
A man lives in the house he plays with the serpents
    he writes
he writes when dusk falls to Germany your golden
    hair Margarete
your ashen hair Shulamith we dig a grave in the
    breezes there one lies unconfined.

---

[2] **fugue**—a musical composition based on one or more short themes in
which different voices or instruments repeat the same melody with slight
variations.

He calls out jab deeper into the earth you lot you
    others sing now and play
he grabs at the iron in his belt he waves it his eyes
    are blue
jab deeper you lot with your spades you others play
    on for the dance

Black milk of daybreak we drink you at night
we drink you at noon in the morning we drink you at
    sundown
we drink you and we drink you
a man lives in the house your golden hair Margarete
your ashen hair Shulamith he plays with the
    serpents

He calls out more sweetly play death death is a
    master from Germany
he calls out more darkly now stroke your strings then
    as smoke you will rise into air
then a grave you will have in the clouds there one
    lies unconfined

Black milk of daybreak we drink you at night
we drink you at noon death is a master from
    Germany
we drink you at sundown and in the morning we drink
    and we drink you
death is a master from Germany his eyes are blue
he strikes you with leaden bullets his aim is true
a man lives in the house your golden hair Margarete
he sets his pack on to us he grants us a grave in the
    air
he plays with the serpents and daydreams death is
    a master from Germany

your golden hair Margarete
your ashen hair Shulamith

Smoke

JACOB GLATSTEIN

Through **crematorium**[3] chimneys
a Jew curls toward the God of his fathers.
As soon as the smoke is gone,
upward cluster his wife and son.

Upward, toward the heavens,
sacred smoke weeps, yearns.
God—where You are—
we all disappear.

---

[3] **crematorium**—furnace for cremating, or burning dead bodies to ashes.

QUESTIONS TO CONSIDER

1. In "If I Only Knew," what do almost all of the items the speaker mentions have in common? What do they symbolize?

2. In "Death Fugue," the image of the grave is repeated throughout the poem. How does the image change from stanza to stanza?

3. What attitude toward death is expressed in the poem "Smoke"?

The Shawl

BY CYNTHIA OZICK

For survivors of the Holocaust, writing represents the challenge of expressing the inexpressible, finding words that are adequate to describe their experiences. For writers who did not experience the Holocaust, writing about it is the entirely different act of imagining life during this time. Cynthia Ozick (1928–) is an American writer who has written extensively about Jewish life. Her short story "The Shawl" is an attempt at just such an imaging of the Holocaust. She creates an experience in a concentration camp and examines the event's importance. Ozick's work is part of the next generation's response to the Holocaust.

Stella, cold, cold, the coldness of hell. How they walked on the roads together, Rosa with Magda curled up between sore breasts, Magda wound up in the shawl. Sometimes Stella carried Magda. But she was jealous of Magda. A thin girl of fourteen, too small, with thin breasts of her own, Stella wanted to be wrapped in a shawl, hidden away, asleep, rocked by the march, a baby, a round infant in arms. Magda took Rosa's nipple, and Rosa never stopped walking, a walking cradle.

There was not enough milk; sometimes Magda sucked air; then she screamed. Stella was ravenous. Her knees were tumors on sticks, her elbows chicken bones.

Rosa did not feel hunger; she felt light, not like someone walking but like someone in a faint, in trance, arrested in a fit, someone who is already a floating angel, alert and seeing everything, but in the air, not there, not touching the road. As if teetering on the tips of her fingernails. She looked into Magda's face through a gap in the shawl: a squirrel in a nest, safe, no one could reach her inside the little house of the shawl's windings. The face, very round, a pocket mirror of a face: but it was not Rosa's bleak complexion, dark like **cholera**,[1] it was another kind of face altogether, eyes blue as air, smooth feathers of hair nearly as yellow as the Star sewn into Rosa's coat. You could think she was one of *their* babies.

Rosa, floating, dreamed of giving Magda away in one of the villages. She could leave the line for a minute and push Magda into the hands of any woman on the side of the road. But if she moved out of line they might shoot. And even if she fled the line for half a second and pushed the shawl-bundle at a stranger, would the woman take it? She might be surprised, or afraid; she might drop the shawl, and Magda would fall out and strike her head and die. The little round head. Such a good child, she gave up screaming, and sucked now only for the taste of the drying nipple itself The neat grip of the tiny gums. One mite of a tooth tip sticking up in the bottom gum, how shining, an elfin tombstone of white marble gleaming there. Without complaining, Magda relinquished Rosa's teats, first the left, then the right; both were cracked, not a sniff of milk. The duct-crevice extinct, a dead volcano, blind eye, chill hole, so Magda took the corner of the shawl and milked it

---

[1] **cholera**—an acute, infectious, often fatal disease of the stomach and intestines.

instead. She sucked and sucked, flooding the threads with wetness. The shawl's good flavor, milk of linen.

It was a magic shawl, it could nourish an infant for three days and three nights. Magda did not die, she stayed alive, although very quiet. A peculiar smell, of cinnamon and almonds, lifted out of her mouth. She held her eyes open every moment, forgetting how to blink or nap, and Rosa and sometimes Stella studied their blueness. On the road they raised one burden of a leg after another and studied Magda's face. "Aryan,"[2] Stella said, in a voice grown as thin as a string; and Rosa thought how Stella gazed at Magda like a young cannibal. And the time that Stella said "Aryan," it sounded to Rosa as if Stella had really said "Let us devour her."

But Magda lived to walk. She lived that long, but she did not walk very well, partly because she was only fifteen months old, and partly because the spindles of her legs could not hold up her fat belly. It was fat with air, full and round. Rosa gave almost all her food to Magda, Stella gave nothing; Stella was ravenous, a growing child herself, but not growing much. Stella did not menstruate. Rosa did not menstruate. Rosa was ravenous, but also not; she learned from Magda how to drink the taste of a finger in one's mouth. They were in a place without pity, all pity was **annihilated**[3] in Rosa, she looked at Stella's bones without pity. She was sure that Stella was waiting for Magda to die so she could put her teeth into the little thighs.

Rosa knew Magda was going to die very soon; she should have been dead already, but she had been buried away deep inside the magic shawl, mistaken there for the shivering mound of Rosa's breasts; Rosa clung to the shawl as if it covered only herself. No one took it away from her. Magda was mute. She never cried. Rosa hid

---

[2] Aryan—term used by the Nazis to describe Caucasian non-Jews.

[3] **annihilated**—destroyed completely; wiped out of existence.

her in the barracks, under the shawl, but she knew that one day someone would inform; or one day someone, not even Stella, would steal Magda to eat her. When Magda began to walk Rosa knew that Magda was going to die very soon, something would happen. She was afraid to fall asleep; she slept with the weight of her thigh on Magda's body; she was afraid she would smother Magda under her thigh. The weight of Rosa was becoming less and less; Rosa and Stella were slowly turning into air.

Magda was quiet, but her eyes were horribly alive, like blue tigers. She watched. Sometimes she laughed—it seemed a laugh, but how could it be? Magda had never seen anyone laugh. Still, Magda laughed at her shawl when the wind blew its corners, the bad wind with pieces of black in it, that made Stella's and Rosa's eyes tear. Magda's eyes were always clear and tearless. She watched like a tiger. She guarded her shawl. No one could touch it; only Rosa could touch it. Stella was not allowed. The shawl was Magda's own baby, her pet, her little sister. She tangled herself up in it and sucked on one of the corners when she wanted to be very still.

Then Stella took the shawl away and made Magda die.

Afterward Stella said: "I was cold."

And afterward she was always cold, always. The cold went into her heart: Rosa saw that Stella's heart was cold. Magda flopped onward with her little pencil legs scribbling this way and that, in search of the shawl; the pencils faltered at the barracks opening, where the light began. Rosa saw and pursued. But already Magda was in the square outside the barracks, in the jolly light. It was the roll-call arena. Every morning Rosa had to conceal Magda under the shawl against a wall of the barracks and go out and stand in the arena with Stella and hundreds of others, sometimes for hours, and Magda, deserted, was quiet under the shawl, sucking on her corner. Every day Magda was silent, and so she did not die. Rosa saw that today Magda was going to die, and at the same time a fearful joy ran in Rosa's two palms, her fingers were on fire, she was astonished, **febrile:**[4] Magda, in the sunlight, swaying on her pencil legs, was howling. Ever since the drying up of Rosa's nipples, ever since Magda's last scream on the road, Magda had been devoid of any syllable; Magda was a mute. Rosa believed that something had gone wrong with her vocal cords, with her windpipe, with the cave of her larynx; Magda was defective, without a voice; perhaps she was deaf; there might be something amiss with her intelligence; Magda was dumb. Even the laugh that came when the ash-stippled wind made a clown out of Magda's shawl was only the air-blown showing of her teeth. Even when the lice, head lice and body lice, crazed her so that she became as wild as one of the big rats that plundered the barracks at daybreak looking for **carrion,**[5] she rubbed and scratched and kicked and bit and rolled without a whimper. But now Magda's mouth was spilling a long **viscous**[6] rope of clamor.

"Maaaa—"

It was the first noise Magda had ever sent out from her throat since the drying up of Rosa's nipples.

"Maaaa . . . aaa!"

Again! Magda was wavering in the perilous sunlight of the arena, scribbling on such pitiful little bent shins. Rosa saw. She saw that Magda was grieving for the loss of her shawl, she saw that Magda was going to die. A tide of commands hammered in Rosa's nipples: Fetch, get, bring! But she did not know which to go after first, Magda or the shawl. If she jumped out into the arena to snatch Magda up, the howling would not stop, because Magda would still not have the shawl; but if she

---

[4] **febrile**—feverish.

[5] **carrion**—dead and decaying flesh.

[6] **viscous**—thick like heavy syrup.

ran back into the barracks to find the shawl, and if she found it, and if she came after Magda holding it and shaking it, then she would get Magda back, Magda would put the shawl in her mouth and turn dumb again.

Rosa entered the dark. It was easy to discover the shawl. Stella was heaped under it, asleep in her thin bones. Rosa tore the shawl free and flew—she could fly, she was only air—into the arena. The sunheat murmured of another life, of butterflies in summer. The light was placid, mellow. On the other side of the steel fence, far away, there were green meadows speckled with dandelions and deep-colored violets; beyond them, even farther, innocent tiger lilies, tall, lifting their orange bonnets. In the barracks they spoke of "flowers," of "rain": excrement, thick turd-braids, and the slow stinking maroon waterfall that slunk down from the upper bunks, the stink mixed with a bitter fatty floating smoke that greased Rosa's skin. She stood for an instant at the margin of the arena. Sometimes the electricity inside the fence would seem to hum; even Stella said it was only an imagining, but Rosa heard real sounds in the wire: grainy sad voices. The farther she was from the fence, the more clearly the voices crowded at her. The lamenting voices strummed so convincingly, so passionately, it was impossible to suspect them of being phantoms. The voices told her to hold up the shawl, high; the voices told her to shake it, to whip with it, to unfurl it like a flag. Rosa lifted, shook, whipped, unfurled. Far off, very far, Magda leaned across her air-fed belly, reaching out with the rods of her arms. She was high up, elevated, riding someone's shoulder. But the shoulder that carried Magda was not coming toward Rosa and the shawl, it was drifting away, the speck of Magda was moving more and more into the smoky distance. Above the shoulder a helmet glinted. The light tapped the helmet and sparkled it into a goblet. Below the helmet a black body like a domino and a pair of black boots hurled themselves in the direction of the electrified fence. The electric voices began to chatter wildly. "Maamaa, maaa-maaa," they all hummed together. How far Magda was from Rosa now, across the whole square, past a dozen barracks, all the way on the other side! She was no bigger than a moth.

All at once Magda was swimming through the air. The whole of Magda traveled through loftiness. She looked like a butterfly touching a silver vine. And the moment Magda's feathered round head and her pencil legs and balloonish belly and zigzag arms splashed against the fence, the steel voices went mad in their growling, urging Rosa to run and run to the spot where Magda had fallen from her flight against the electrified fence; but of course Rosa did not obey them. She only stood, because if she ran they would shoot, and if she tried to pick up the sticks of Magda's body they would shoot, and if she let the wolf's screech ascending now through the ladder of her skeleton break out, they would shoot; so she took Magda's shawl and filled her own mouth with it, stuffed it in and stuffed it in, until she was swallowing up the wolf's screech and tasting the cinnamon and almond depth of Magda's saliva; and Rosa drank Magda's shawl until it dried.

QUESTIONS TO CONSIDER

1. What is the conflict between Rosa and Stella?

2. Why does Rosa not go after Magda? What do her actions convey about life in the camp?

3. What do you think the shawl in the story symbolizes?

1988

BY VALERIE JAKOBER FURTH

Valerie Jakober Furth (1926–) was born in Czechoslovakia into an Orthodox Jewish family. The Germans occupied Czechoslovakia in 1939, and Jewish families immediately felt the full weight of Nazi policies. In 1944, Furth's entire family was sent to Auschwitz. Thirty-six members of the family died before the camp was evacuated in January 1945. In 1988, the Simon Wiesenthal Center, which sponsors an annual trip to Auschwitz, asked Furth as a survivor to accompany a group going to see the remains of the camps, which are now a memorial. "1988" is Furth's account of her journey back.

This year I returned to Auschwitz. However, now I stayed only six hours, on a cold and dreary March afternoon. I came with sixteen other people, including my husband, who were part of a tour sponsored by the Simon Wiesenthal Center. The tour is a yearly affair, and the center tries on each trip to take at least one survivor of the death camps. Of our group, I was that survivor.

Why had I decided to return? In the months after I finally told the center to include us on the trip, this question flitted in and out of my head. I answered it by saying that my art was at a standstill: on the one hand, when I painted the Holocaust, something was missing. On the other hand, when I tried to escape from my experience, I made pretty pictures. Neither was an acceptable possibility. Perhaps I needed to rekindle my anger at what had happened to me and those I had loved at Auschwitz and the other camps. Lately, I had felt it diminishing, and though in one way this was good, I also felt that there were still too many blanks in my memory. If I were really to come to terms with Auschwitz, then I needed to confront it again.

These were the reasons I gave myself for going in the months before our departure, when I thought at all about what I had embarked on. Most of the time, however, life flowed on comfortably, and what awaited me seemed far away.

On the one-hour bus trip from Cracow to Auschwitz, my feelings changed. I had been asked by Rhonda, the director of the Wiesenthal Center in New York, who accompanied us, to say a few words. Back in the hotel, the speech I had prepared seemed quite satisfactory, but now on the bus I had difficulty speaking because, as we sped through the countryside, pictures of camp life began, like photographs in a darkroom, to enlarge in my mind. And as they succeeded one another in a silent progression, I wanted desperately to feel what I had felt when I first passed through the gates of Auschwitz—as I stood waiting on endless lines to use the latrines, as I lay huddled on my bunk in Barrack C. So, instead of my prepared speech, I said a few words and sat down.

We passed through the gate. Had there been brick buildings in that Auschwitz? All the structures I remembered had been of wood. No, this is not where I had lived and most of my family had died. But there was the crematorium chimney, the look-out towers (but hadn't they been wooden too?), and the barbed wire. Where was I? Meanwhile, the young Polish woman who was our guide had joined us and began talking. She was cool, detached, brisk, and I disliked her immediately. Her voice and manner grated on me. How dare she talk statistics; it was my brother, my nephews, my aunts she was reducing to numbers. (On the night before, I had counted up thirty-six members of my immediate family who had died in the camps.) Impatiently, I broke into the guide's patter.

"Where was C Camp, Barracks 26?" I asked. Her smooth progression interrupted, she became annoyed.

"Camp C was in Birkenau. We'll go there after the museum."

Two other groups were in the dark cool museum with us: a crowd of German tourists and some Hasidim[1] from Israel. A map showed three camps. It was then I recalled that where we had just entered was not the place where I and my family had arrived. The site of the museum had originally housed political prisoners. Until this moment, I had never realized that Camp C, Barracks 26 had been a part of Birkenau.

I asked our guide where the kitchen was on the map. She showed it to me. When I said that I would like to see it, she answered that we would go there after the museum. I had seen many of the pictures on the walls of the museum, but was unprepared for the rush of emotion I felt on looking at the glass cases filled with human hair, toothbrushes, shoes, and suitcases of the camp's inmates. My Aunt Ida's hair, my cousin Nellie's toothbrush, the hiking shoes I had worn at arrival, the backpack my mother carried with her to camp. . . . Were they somewhere in these desolate piles of human debris?

Our last stop in the museum was the small room of eternal light. As I knelt down and lit candles, their flames

---

[1] Hasidim—members of a Jewish sect founded in the 1700s in Poland. Hasidim believe in mysticism and emphasize religious piety and devotion over formal learning.

came up and with them, my life in the Auschwitz inferno rose up too, the flames licking but not burning the images of lost ones from my mind. I felt my husband's hand on my shoulder. Deeply affected, he too was mourning the death of loved ones—the father and stepmother who had vanished in the Nazi night.

After the museum, we got on the bus for our ride to Birkenau. Once again, we entered through an iron gate, but this time I knew where I was. A field, wooden barracks, a brick chimney told me that, after nearly forty years, I had found the way back to my Auschwitz.

Again, I asked the guide, "Where is the kitchen? Where is Camp C?"

She replied that nothing remained of Camp C except some brick chimneys.

"Can we go there anyway?"

"Impossible, the gates are locked. We can, however, see the ruins of the crematorium."

Nothing to be done. As we approached the ruins, the forest, used by the Nazis as a holding place when the crematorium was too full, loomed menacingly. Nearby, I glimpsed a lake, the same lake into which the ashes of the dead had been dumped. But it was Camp C, not them, that holds my attention. I try to zoom in on it with my camera.

"Can we go to the barracks in Camp A?" I ask, already anticipating the No that is the answer.

"We don't have time," the guide says. But, after I tell Rhonda I am not leaving until we stand on that ground, and she had a whispered conversation with the guide, it is decided that we will see the barracks after all.

It is not Barracks 26, Camp C, but all the barracks were identical in their arrangement and structure, so I will have to be content, and as I stand on the barracks floor, for the first time since we arrived I am no longer a tourist. I am cold and hungry; my mother is talking to me with a worried look on her face about food, recipes.

She is praying, she is crying, "Where are my sisters, my brothers?" Beside her, I am vowing, "I won't die, and I won't let her die."

I came back to reality. Now I know why I have returned to Auschwitz: to make sure that what happened to me forty years ago was not a dream, to renew the pledge I made in my art: to grip those who see my work so that they will remember what happened to us and never let it happen again. I look around me at the wooden slats that once held my shivering body. I am ready to leave.

But that night in the hotel room, my head spins with images. One that recurs is of the ditch where I used to get water to wash after it had rained. There had been a rag. How had I ever acquired it? My possessions had been reduced to zero. This small rag was half the size of a handkerchief. I had used it as my washcloth, towel and pillow case.

Theresienstadt, which we visited three days later, looked civil in contrast to Auschwitz. The sky was blue, and we had a new guide—a middle-aged Czech with a human face. Though we were never shown the part of the camp where the Jews were housed, I was not so angry as I had been with the Polish accountant. By the fake cemetery which the Nazis had built to hide the fact that no bodies slept underneath the headstones—for all that remained of these dead were their ashes—we read aloud poems written by the children of Theresienstadt. In this peaceful setting of death, their clear voices, alive to the world's beauty, were unbearably moving.

It is almost a month since I have returned home. Since then, I have wakened each morning with a great heaviness in my body. One day I identify this feeling: It is how I used to feel lying pressed against my mother on the wooden slats that were our beds in Auschwitz.

I have returned home. Patiently, I wait to see how my art will contain the answers to the questions that set me forth on this painful journey back.

1. Why did Furth decide to go on the tour of Auschwitz?

2. What most affected Furth on her visit to Auschwitz? What about those sights and items affected her so strongly?

Buried Homeland

BY AHARON APPELFELD

*Aharon Appelfeld (1932–) is one of Israel's foremost writers.
Born in Czernovitz in what is now Romania, Appelfeld, as a child,
experienced the brutal effects of the Nazi occupation. In 1940,
his father was sent to a concentration camp and his mother murdered. Appelfeld escaped from a camp and spent three years in
hiding from the Nazi occupiers. In 1946, he was able to immigrate
to Palestine, to the region that would become the state of Israel
in 1948. As an Israeli, he was unable to travel to his homeland
which became part of the Soviet Union after World War II.
However, after the collapse of Soviet rule in 1989, the restrictions
were lifted and in 1996 Appelfeld returned to the region he grew
up in. His essay "Buried Homeland" recounts that journey.*

For years, I dreamed about going back to my childhood home, but I didn't, because after the war the
region belonged to the Soviet Union and, as an Israeli,
I would not have been allowed to enter it. The dream
slowly faded, and I reconciled myself to the thought
that I would never again see the place where I came into
the world.

Then, in 1989, something unbelievable happened: the vast and mighty Soviet Empire collapsed, and the gates were opened. Holocaust survivors who had yearned for years to see their old homeland now thronged the doors of consulates to obtain visas. They knew that no one was expecting them, but still they crowded together and stood in line for hours.

I was in no hurry to join them. Over the years, after arriving in Israel, in 1946, I gradually realized that returning home after a long period of separation was not a simple matter. Years ago, I wrote a novella in which I described the reunion of a man and wife who had been separated by the war for two decades: Instead of joy and love, there arose suspicion and estrangement. Some of that sense of estrangement clung to me whenever I thought of returning.

I was driven away from home at the age of eight and a half. What does a child of eight and a half remember? Almost nothing. But, miraculously, that "almost nothing" has nourished me for years. Not a day passes when I'm not at home. In my adopted country of Israel, I have written thirty books that draw directly or indirectly upon the village of my childhood, whose name is found only on ordnance maps. That "almost nothing" is the well from which I draw and draw, and it seems that there is no end to its waters.

Sometimes I think that this great plenty has come to me because I was an only child and my parents lavished upon me what others give to three children. They walked with me in the mountains until twilight and read me books, some of which I understood and most of which were beyond my understanding, and on summer nights my mother and I used to sit, contemplating the sky and listening to the silence. As soon as I was able to walk by myself, I was drawn to the green shade of the Carpathian[1] forests. In those days, I didn't know that

---

[1] Carpathian—part of a mountain system of central Europe, extending in an arc from central Czechoslovakia to southwest Romania.

Hasidism, the great mystical movement in Judaism, arose in those eternal forests.

That marvellous life lasted for eight and a half years, but in June, 1941, it was cut off with a mighty clap of thunder. Germans and Romanians invaded the village, and, with the cooperation of the local population, they slaughtered most of its Jewish inhabitants. My mother and grandmother were among the slain. The invaders used old methods: they shot a few to death and butchered many more. Shouts and sobs filled the village for two days, and they continue to arouse me from my sleep.

Another life began—a life without my mother. My father and I ran away from the village, to the ghetto in Czernovitz. Later, soldiers rounded us up and drove us to the camps in Transnistria. First our lives were embittered with hunger, then with cold. I was separated from my father, left alone with the hungry women and children, and was consumed by the visions of death that had already infected so many other people. Children who were playing "five stones" on the cement floor at night were found frozen to death the next morning.

Who extricated me and bore me back to life? I don't know. Sometimes it seems to me that my mother, who often appeared in my dreams, whispered to me to get up and go. About those blind and tortured years, when I was a child, wandering from village to village, frightened but determined to survive, I have hardly written. Indeed, I have written very little about the war in general. In war, the body shrinks and the soul fades; hunger and cold take control of you. In the end, your life is compacted into a single desire: to die as quickly as possible.

In 1996, it became clear to me that I could no longer put off my return home. An old feeling of guilt, which I had repressed for many years, floated up. Its essence was a mass grave in the village of Drajinetz, in which my mother and grandmother were buried. The thought that one day I might stand by that grave in silence would not leave me. I am not an observant Jew, but my connection with the faith of my fathers has always been deep. I inherited it from my mother. My mother was not observant either, but her belief in the spiritual—though she didn't use that word—was fervent and clear, seeming to say that the circle of life is wider than we imagine. That sense of the world, which was embodied in her silent gaze, haunted me, and I very much wanted to connect with her life in the place where it had come to an end more than fifty years ago, when she was thirty-three and I was eight and a half.

Everybody discouraged me from going there. Ukraine, I was told, was engulfed in anarchy: the mafia ruled, and travel to the villages was dangerous. But those warnings only strengthened my resolve, and it was strengthened all the more when I heard, earlier this year, that a crew from Israeli educational television was going to the region to photograph the cemeteries, the remains of the camps, and the mass graves. I immediately asked to join the expedition. The group included my wife, Judith; Yitzhak Artzi, who came from the region and had done a great deal to save Jews during the war; his daughter, the writer Nava Semel; two senior staff members from Yad Vashem, the Israeli Holocaust Memorial institution; and the television crew. The realization that my private tragedy was bound up with the great tragedy of the Jewish people drew me out of my shell. Although I am a child of modern literature, in which the individual is the chief concern, I feel that were it not for my ties to the Jews and to Judaism my individuality would be shallow.

We flew to Bucharest, and from there we made our way to the Ukrainian border along roads that could scarcely be described as roads. We immediately felt the heavy hand of the Ukrainian bureaucracy: customs officials examined our documents and our equipment for five hours, and we reached Czernovitz at midnight.

The city lay half in darkness, but I could nevertheless see that it wasn't the city I had known. Ugly new houses stood row upon row, an inheritance from the Communist regime. This was not my Czernovitz, along whose avenues I had loved to stroll with my parents, and where I had spent the happiest hours of my life. Fatigue now rescued me, as it sometimes does, and I sank into deep sleep. I dreamed about nothing, as though I wished to flee this place.

The next morning, we left our modern hotel, which had been built under the Communists, and strolled to the center of town. To my surprise, the center was as I remembered it. Signs of neglect were everywhere, but from the neglect peered evidence of the beauty of Little Vienna, as Czernovitz had been called in the good, tranquil days of the Hapsburg monarchy.[2] Herrengasse, the street of fashionable clothing stores, restaurants, and cafés, was not what it had been, but beneath the peeling walls one could see delicate traces of the old elegance. The familiar buildings were still in place: the Black Eagle Hotel, the city hall, the theatre, the Jewish theatre, the splendid university. A child's eyes had looked upon them with wonder, many years ago. Now, although the magic was gone, every street corner reminded me of an outing with my parents, a surprising gift, the fresh breezes of summer, the fragrance of flowers from a flower shop, and my father's invitation "Let's go to Café Europa."

A childhood city is an ideal city. Czernovitz had always been a holiday for me. I had seen broad, freshly washed sidewalks, iron fences that were works of art, the shadows of chestnut trees. Along its streets I had looked into display windows, and into cafés lit up in Viennese style—cafés where my parents had coffee and strudel and I was served a generous portion of ice

---

[2] Hapsburg monarchy—from the 15th–20th centuries, the Hapsburg family headed one of the most prominent dynasties in Europe. In 1867, the monarchy took form as Austria-Hungary.

cream. Ever since then, when I have written about a city, it has been Czernovitz.

If Czernovitz is the model city for me, Drajinetz is my model village. When I was a month old, I was brought there from Zadova, and I lived in Drajinetz for more than eight years. My mother's beautiful face was revealed to me there, and it was there that she was snatched from me.

Our house in Drajinetz had double-glazed windows during the winter to keep in the warmth; in the spring, the inner panes were removed. There were window boxes full of red flowers; big glass doors, which trans- ferred the light from room to room; and broad-shoul- dered Ruthenian servant women. In summer, I played in the courtyard, and I used to sit for hours watching a hen pecking or a long-necked goose tensely shielding her goslings. Who could have imagined that in this village, on a Saturday, our Sabbath, sixty-two souls, most of them women and children, would fall prey to pitchforks and kitchen knives, and I, because I was in a back room, would manage to escape to the cornfields and hide?

For years, that village lay within me, and now I was approaching it. I couldn't find anything recognizable about it. All the buildings were low, enveloped in shadows and vines, and looked like one another. Signs said "Drajinetz," but I couldn't identify anything famil- iar. It was noon, and the young people I encountered apparently didn't know that Jews had ever lived there. Perhaps they were feigning ignorance. Judith and I met an old man in a wheelchair, which he propelled with his hands. He must have been in the village when my fam- ily lived there, but he was hurrying to the doctor and wouldn't speak with us. Another old man came toward us. He remembered the Jews—he even mentioned two names—but he had never heard about the slaughter. The villagers surrounded us. I remembered those faces:

a mixture of cunning, suspicion, and false innocence. The answers they gave were **convoluted**,[3] and it was hard to know what was true and what was made up.

"Where is the mass grave?" I asked with the help of an interpreter. No one knew. Suddenly the sob of the slaughter rose within me—the sob I hear at night—and it made me dizzy. Raising my voice, I said, "I lived here until the age of eight and a half, and I know that Jews were slaughtered here." No response. I felt the villagers' stares on my body.

Approximately a hundred Jews had lived in the village, most of them merchants. After the slaughter, their houses were plundered. It struck me that some treasures of ours must still be hidden in those houses. Maybe my books. Maybe my parents' library, my grandmother's prayer books.

The peasants looked at me with tense expressions. Perhaps I had come to claim property, or to look for old Nazi collaborators. Peasants in this region have always been wary—you can't discover their thoughts easily. Suddenly, one of them turned to me and asked, "What do you remember from then?" Not very much, I wanted to say, but I restrained myself. My delay in replying brought a smile to the man's lips, and he said, "See, you've also forgotten."

I was discouraged. For a moment, it seemed to me that I had come here by mistake—that this was no longer my village. Perhaps it had changed so drastically that no vestiges of it remained. I raised my eyes, and some distance away I saw a two-story brick building and, opposite it, a church. I had no further doubt: this was the village. I had finished first grade in that brick building, and on Sundays and holidays people in the village had streamed into that church. One summer, there was a drought, and I could remember a procession leaving the church, bearing images and headed by the

---

[3] **convoluted**—complicated; intricate.

priest. My self-assurance returned. Everyone agreed that the brick building had once served as a school.

In my journal, years ago, I tried to reconstruct that school year:

> We were two Jewish children—in a class of forty peasant children. I was thin and was dressed in delicate clothes and my mother escorted me to the gate. That escort did not bring me much honor. During recess, all the children played with a red rubber ball in the yard, raising dust and yelling. I used to stand at the window and watch. Even then, I apparently knew that I would never play freely, like them. The feeling was painful, but it was also amusing, a mixture of inferiority and superiority. I could amuse myself in my thoughts as long as I was beyond the other children's reach. In their presence I was a target for kicks, slaps, or pinches.
>
> They were taller and sturdier than I was. I knew that even if I exerted all my strength I couldn't narrow the gap. They would always rule the corridor and the schoolyard. On a whim, they beat you or left you alone. Sometimes when I sensed an attack coming, I would stand on the stone stairs and yell at the top of my lungs, mostly to overcome my fear.
>
> Mother tried to intervene with the principal Her effort was useless. Forty sturdy bodies were opposed to me, a mighty torrent of legs that swept aside everything that stood in their way, including me. Several times, I tried to defend myself. That made no impression on the gang. On the contrary, by claiming that I had started it they now had even more reason to hit me. The other Jewish boy had abandoned me in the battle. Soon, he changed completely. Even though he was thinner than I was, he fitted well into the games in the schoolyard. What he couldn't do

by strength was done by agility. After a while, he turned his back on me, as though he were no longer a member of the tribe.

Day after day, from the early morning hours, and in the winter, from the dark morning hours, until two in the afternoon, I was in the company of that wild herd, and is it any wonder that I don't remember a single name—not even that of the pale-faced teacher, who was Jewish? She struggled with that mass of people, who, at the age of seven, were already full of the urge to destroy. This teacher stood by helplessly, shouting in vain and provoking waves of laughter. I don't remember faces, but I remember the broad stone stairs very well and the dark, humid hallway, with the flood of legs sliding down and galloping out.

In all that fear, the only consolation I had was the malicious joy I felt when the school's janitors disciplined the other children. These two old men roamed around the corridors and the courtyard like quiet and cunning agents of justice. If a boy acted up, they would seize him and give him ten lashes, and if he was impudent they would add another five more. The victim, after receiving his punishment, had to kiss the hand of the man who had beaten him and say, "As you command, Father." Then the boy would clear out. That was the ceremony, and it was repeated several times every week. Because I was a polite, obedient boy, the janitors never beat me. I was beaten by the other boys. Malicious joy was my only joy in that place.

Fifty-seven years had passed since then, and the memory of that prolonged indignity had not been erased from my heart. Now I stood in the courtyard of that school—a courtyard that no longer had walls—

surrounded by the village people. I am a native of this place, I told them, perhaps to remind them that I had a certain moral right to be there, or perhaps to remind myself of that.

I left the courtyard and turned in the direction of my parents' house. Two newer houses now occupied its place. But it appeared that my father's flour mill was still there—smaller than it had been. My father's mill had burned down, the villagers explained, and been replaced by a smaller one. I circled the mill to see whether any of the original structure remained, and I noticed that the foundations had not been disturbed.

More peasants gathered. They inspected me, and I inspected them. "Who remembers the Appelfeld family?" I asked. When they understood my question, a tremor passed among them. One of the old men approached me and said, "It's hard to remember family names. We remember given names." I said nothing. For some reason, it was hard for me to mention the names of my father and mother.

Then a tall man, dressed in city clothes, appeared. He asked why the crowd had gathered. The peasants explained that I had been asking questions. I told him my family name. The man looked at me alertly and exclaimed, "You're Erwin Appelfeld!" He went on to say, "Your mother's name was Bunya, and your father was Michael. I studied in school with you. Do you remember me?"

I couldn't breathe. The man asked how many children I had and where I lived. Hearing that I had three children and that I lived in Jerusalem, he burst into tears. Now it was clear to everyone: I was not a chance visitor. Even so, the villagers were reluctant to tell me where the mass grave was. "The Jews were slaughtered here," I declared again. Again, there was no response.

A tall peasant came up, and, as if in an old ceremony, the village people explained to him what I wanted to know. He raised his arm and pointed: it was over there, on a hill. There was silence, then an outpouring of speech, which I could not understand.

It turned out that what the people of the village had tried to conceal from me was well known, even to the children. I asked several little children, who were standing near the fence and looking at us, where the Jews' graves were. Right away, they raised their hands and pointed.

As we climbed the hill, a glorious landscape greeted us: the Carpathian Mountains, in their full splendor. Here people still tilled the land as they had done for generations, without machinery. The hoe, the pitchfork, and the horse-drawn plow were their tools. The cultivated fields were a green, yellow, and red mosaic. The distant mountains cast dark-blue shadows on the nearer hilltops. Nothing prevented peace and beauty from dwelling here.

The villagers walked at our side, as though to see what mischief we might do. I asked them what they remembered from the times when Jews lived here. They were stingy with their words, but finally one of them said, "Here's the grave." He pointed at an uncultivated field.

"Are you sure?" I asked.

"I buried them," the peasant replied. He added, "I was sixteen."

A book of psalms that I had brought along rescued me from muteness. I opened it and read the first psalm. Two members of the Israeli television crew joined me in reciting the Kaddish.[4] Upon hearing the prayers, the peasants withdrew. We stood in silence. Many thoughts raced through my mind, but none that I could grasp. My mother's face, whose features I had preserved for so many years, was suddenly erased from my memory. I looked at the peasants. They stared back, as if wondering what I was going to say. Some of the women began to weep, but no one approached me.

---

[4] Kaddish—a prayer praising God that is recited by Jewish mourners.

Once again, I asked an old peasant what he remembered from that time. "I don't remember much," he said, and he placed his hand on his chest. Then he said that he did remember our neighbor Mr. Saler, who owned a grocery store—that he used to buy candy from him.

Walking down the hill, I felt a strong desire to stay in the village, to go from house to house and ask what people remembered of the old days, but I knew that even if I were to stay there for a month I would discover nothing new. If the Jews had once appeared to the peasants as servants of Satan, they were now ghosts who rose from the mass graves scattered among the villages. I had heard about that fear. The rabbi in Czernovitz had told us that Ruthenian peasant women came to him to ask not only for advice or a blessing but also for forgiveness for what the Ukrainians did to the Jews. In Czernovitz, we had found many church candles placed on the graves of famous rabbis. It seemed that, even though no Jews remained in the city, their spirits wandered about everywhere, and must be appeased.

Every town or village had a neglected Jewish cemetery and, not far away, a mass grave. In a short time, those traces would vanish, and the region would be not only without Jews but without any memory of them. The tragedy of the Holocaust is epitomized by, among other things, the inability to grasp its enormity. I knew that, but now it was driven home to me. Strange, how little we have to say in the presence of death. Even a believer stands mute. Mass deaths fill us with a feeling of horror and despair—even worse, with indifference.

To extricate myself from the abyss of silence, I held fast, once again, to the memory of my mother in that little village of Drajinetz, where the world was revealed to me in trees, water, and blossoming fields: my mother and father in the living room or the broad kitchen, with their belief that the good and the beautiful were boundless.

We made our bumpy way back to the Romanian border. Again, I came upon the ravishing landscape of my homeland. Only then did the feeling that I had been at my mother's grave grip me. I am sixty-six years old—twice her age when she died. The thought that she would always remain young and beautiful and I would grow old alongside her youth filled me with pain and wonder.

Until recently, I had thought that there existed a childhood home far from me and another childhood home within me. Now I know: what there was dwells only within me. Outside is an alien land, like my village, which has uprooted the memory of the common life of the past hundred and fifty years without leaving a trace. The synagogue in that village had been erased, and not even a small marker in memory of the slaughtered had been erected. The silent peasants who gathered around me would certainly have preferred that I hadn't come. My presence had aroused fear and repugnance. What could I have said to them? That I understood them, that I forgave them? The truth is that I felt neither anger nor the desire for revenge. I had been enveloped in sorrow for my mother's young life. For years, I had tried to draw her up out of the harsh darkness where she lay. I had failed to redeem her from the alien land and from her imprisonment, but I had seen where she was buried and what you can see from there.

QUESTIONS TO CONSIDER

1. What lessons about war did Appelfeld learn as a result of his childhood experiences?

2. Why were the villagers initially so suspicious of Appelfeld?

3. Why does Appelfeld believe that the regions he visited not only had no Jewish residents, but also harbored no memories of the Jews who once lived there?

ACKNOWLEDGEMENTS

10 "Dedication" from *The Collected Poems: 1931-1987* by Czeslaw Milosz. Copyright © 1988 by Czeslaw Milosz Roylaties, Inc. Reprinted by permission of The Ecco Press.

12 "The Nuremberg Laws" from *Documents of Destruction* edited by Raul Hilberg, Chicago (Quadrangle Books) 1971. Reprinted by permission.

19 *Kristallnacht* from *Never to Forget* by Milton Meltzer. Editor's text copyright © 1976 by Milton Meltzer. (Used by permission of HarperCollins Publishers.)

34 "The Creation of the Ghettos" from *The Holocaust* by Martin Gilbert. Copyright © 1985 by Martin Gilbert. (New York: Holt, Rinehart and Winston, 1986.)

34 "The Creation of the Ghettos" (charts) from *Documents of Destruction* edited by Raul Hilberg, Chicago (Quadrangle Books) 1971. Reprinted by permission.

43 "Life in Lodz" from *Lodz Ghetto* by Alan Adelson and Robert Lapides. Copyright © 1989 by The Jewish Heritage Writing Project. Used by permission of Viking Penguin, a division of Penguin Putnam Inc.

53 "The Last Morning" from *Anton, the Dove Fancier* by Bernard Gotfryd. Reprinted by permission of IMG Literary.

62 *All But My Life* reprinted by permission of Hill and Wang, a division of Farrar, Straus & Giroux, Inc. Excerpt from *All But My Life* by Gerda Weissmann Klein. Copyright © 1957, 1995 by Gerda Weissmann Klein.

74 "1980" by Abraham Sutzkever, translated by Cynthia Ozick from *The Penguin Book of Modern Yiddish Verse* by Irving Howe, Ruth Wisse and Khone Shmeruk. Introduction and Notes Copyright © 1987 by Irving Howe. Used by permission of Viking Penguin, a division of Penguin Putnam Inc.

78 From *A Generation of Wrath* by Elio Romano. Copyright © 1984 by Elio Romano.

89 "The Wannsee Conference" from *The Holocaust* by Martin Gilbert. Copyright © 1985 by Martin Gilbert. (New York: Holt, Rinehart and Winston, 1986.)

101 "One Year in Treblinka" from *The Death Camp Treblinka: A Documentary* by Jankiel Wiernik ed. by Alexander Donat, reprinted with permission from the United States Holocaust Memorial Museum.

109 "The Verdict" from *Auschwitz: True Tales From a Grotesque Land* by Sara Nomberg-Przytyk, edited by Eli Pfefferkorn and David H. Hirsch. Translated by Roslyn Hirsch. Copyright © 1985 by the University of North Carolina Press. Used by permission of the publisher.

115 From *A Man For Others* by Patricia Treece. Copyright © 1982 by Patricia Treece. (New York: HarperCollins)

132 "Chelmno" reprinted with the permission of The Free Press, a Division of Simon & Schuster, Inc. From *The Good Old Days: The Holocaust as Seen by the Perpetrators and Bystanders* by Ernst Klee, Willi Dressen and Volker Riess. Translated by Deborah Burnstone. Copyright © 1988 by S. Verlag GmbH. Translation, Copyright © 1991 by Deborah Burnstone.

140 "Commanding a Concentration Camp" from *Commandant of Auschwitz* by Rudolf Höss.

150 "Liberation" from *Ashes to Life* by Lucille Eichengreen. Copyright © 1994 by Lucille Eichengreen. (San Francisco: Mercury House, 1994.)

157 Excerpt from *Night* by Elie Wiesel, translated by Stella Rodway. Reprinted by permission of Hill and Wang, a division of Farrar, Straus & Giroux, Inc. Copyright © 1960 by MacGibbon & Kee. Copyright renewed © 1988 by The Collins Publishing Group.

161 "Chorus of the Rescued" from *O The Chimneys* by Nelly Sachs, translated by Ruth and Matthew Mead and Michael Roloff. Reprinted by permission of Farrar, Straus & Giroux, Inc. Translation copyright © 1967 and translation copyright renewed © 1995 by Farrar, Straus & Giroux, Inc.

163 "How?" by Abraham Sutzkever from *A. Sutzkever: Selected Poetry and Prose*, translated by Barbara and Benjamin Harshav. Copyright © 1991 by The Regents of the University of California. Reprinted by permisson of the University of California Press.

172 "Shame" reprinted with the permission of Summit Books, a Division of Simon & Schuster, Inc. From *The Drowned and the Saved* by Primo Levi. Translated from the Italian by Raymond Rosenthal. Copyright © 1986 by Giulio Einaudi editore s.p.s., Torino. Translation copyright © 1988 by Simon & Schuster, Inc.

185 "Another Meaning of the Holocaust" from *Surviving and Other Essays* by Bruno Bettelheim. Copyright © 1979 by Bruno Bettelheim and Trude Bettelheim as Trustees. Reprinted by permission of Alfred A. Knopf, Inc.

192 "If I Only Knew" from *O The Chimneys* by Nelly Sachs, translated by Ruth and Matthew Mead and Michael Roloff. Reprinted by permission of Farrar, Straus & Giroux, Inc. Translation copyright © 1967 and translation copyright renewed © 1995 by Farrar, Straus & Giroux, Inc.

193 "Death Fugue" from *Poems of Paul Celan* by Paul Celan translated by Michael Hambuger. Copyright 1995 © by Michael Hambuger. Reprinted by permission of Persea Books, Inc.

195 "Smoke" from *Selected Poem's of Yankev Glatshteyn* by Jacob Glatstein, edited and translated by Richard J. Fein. Used by permission of The Jewish Publication Society.

196 From *The Shawl* by Cynthia Ozick. Copyright © 1980, 1983 by Cynthia Ozick. Reprinted by permission of Alfred A. Knopf, Inc.

203 "1988" from *Cabbages & Geraniums* by Valerie Jakober-Furth. Reprinted by permission of Social Science Monographs, Boulder, Colorado.

209 "Buried Homeland" by Aharon Appelfeld as appeared in *The New Yorker*, November 23, 1998.

Photo Research Diane Hamilton

Photos Courtesy of the Library of Congress and the National Archives.

Every effort has been made to secure complete rights and permissions for each selection presented herein. Updated acknowledgements, if needed, will appear in subsequent printings.

Index